"Debra Moreno Garcia and Wilson Ho have hit the bullseye with this dialectical behavior therapy (DBT) workbook for teens! Written in teen-friendly language with lots of prompts for self-reflection that make it interactive, the authors make the process of developing self-regulation skills fun and accessible, and never preachy or clinical. This workbook could be great for many teens on its own or as an adjunct to a DBT intervention program."

—Jeffrey J. Wood, PhD, professor of education and psychiatry at UCLA, and author of more than 100 articles and chapters on cognitive behavioral interventions and emotional and behavioral development in school-aged youth

"This workbook not only makes the components of DBT easily digestible for therapists and their clients, but does so in an incredibly engaging way. The exercises and tools are useful and easy for folks to utilize outside the session, like the 'e-mantras!' Highly recommend this workbook for any therapist working with teenagers and young adults!"

—Judi Stadler, LCSW, director of clinical services for Para Los Ninos Mental Health Program

"This workbook is a delightful guide, full of important information for adolescents to understand themselves. It is also a great resource for therapists to use with the adolescents they work with."

—Evelyn Lizeth Coria, LCSW, infant-family and early childhood mental health specialist, and Reflective Practice II Facilitator

"*The Dialectical Behavior Therapy Skills Workbook for Teens* is an exceptionally practical book that illuminates the core principle of DBT in a very concise, coherent, and strategic approach. The book contains numerous examples, exercises, and handouts which can be utilized by readers. This book is an excellent guide for teenagers who are dealing with emotional dysregulations. I endorse this book as an additional therapeutic tool for teenagers, parents, and mental health practitioners."

—Iman Dadras, PhD, LMFT, associate professor of couple and family therapy at Alliant International University, Los Angeles

"Moreno Garcia and Ho have a keen understanding of the challenges faced by today's teenagers. *The Dialectical Behavior Therapy Skills Workbook for Teens* dives deep into the topic of stress and its impact on overall well-being. This book is certain to help readers recognize and reflect on stressors, and gain a greater understanding of their own experiences. A great tool for teenagers to begin the journey of improving their well-being."

—Olga Aguilar, MA, LMFT, CEO of Arroyo Seco Family Therapy Inc.

T0051489

SIMPLE SKILLS TO BALANCE EMOTIONS, MANAGE STRESS & FEEL BETTER NOW

DIALECTICAL BEHAVIOR THERAPY SKILLS WORKBOOK FOR TEENS

DEBRA MORENO GARCIA, PHD · WILSON HO, MFT

Instant Help Books
An Imprint of New Harbinger Publications, Inc.

Publisher's Note

INSTANT HELP, the Clock Logo, and NEW HARBINGER are trademarks of New Harbinger Publications, Inc.

New Harbinger Publications is an employee-owned company.

Instant Help Books
An imprint of New Harbinger Publications, Inc.
5720 Shattuck Avenue
Oakland, CA 94609
www.newharbinger.com

Cover design by Amy Shoup

Interior illustrations by Sara Christian

Acquired by Jess O'Brien

Library of Congress Cataloging-in-Publication Data on file

Printed in the United States of America

26   25   24

10   9   8   7   6   5   4   3   2   1   First Printing

This DBT workbook is dedicated to my mom, Teresa Martinez, aka "Granma Terry."
Her relentless support through the years of my every whim (without judgment) has
allowed me to forge new adventures and accomplishments. I owe my bravery to her.

Her perseverance and kind generosity to all she met built encouragement
for those in pursuit of their passions.

With eternal love and gratitude,

Debra & Wilson

CONTENTS

A LETTER TO YOU FROM US

Dear Teenager,

Thanks for opening this book. So, what intrigued you? Seems like there's something you want to dive into to learn more about yourself and how to get through this awesome, yet confusing and stressful thing called life.

By carefully listening to teenagers like yourself, we have learned about the magnitude of adolescent stressors and worries that make life complicated. Adolescents have taught us to understand the heightened levels of stress and accompanying pain and angst you may be experiencing. And you know what? That's okay! This workbook will help you reduce stress, find comfort, and build a sense of belonging on your journey.

We hope this workbook, with examples of diverse life circumstances from other teens, will help connect you to yourself and others—especially since we understand that adults don't always acknowledge teen stress-related issues nor provide meaningful exchanges of support and guidance. You've probably experienced an adult's attempts at good advice turning out to be dismissive, with misinterpretations of your situation. This workbook offers you the chance to tell your own story and write about the changes you want to create for yourself.

Overall, we hope this workbook will help you:

- empower your voice
- build self-advocacy
- improve well-being
- cope with stressors
- develop important life skills
- create meaningful interactions
- manifest a new outcome on your life journey

We want to thank you for letting us guide you through this process of change, discovery, and well-being. We know you can do it!

—Dr. G and Wilson

WHAT IS DIALECTICAL BEHAVIOR THERAPY?

Dialectical behavior therapy (DBT) is a therapeutic approach that has been proven to reduce anger, stress, depression, hostility, and dissociation (Dimeff and Linehan 2001). People who have received this treatment have demonstrated a profound shift in how they feel and have made gains in everyday functioning.

The primary component of DBT is to replace embedded, rigid ways of thinking. This thinking is similar to a term you may have heard before: "all-or-nothing thinking." This is when a person gets stuck in perceiving experiences and challenges as either all good or all bad. As you might know, this can alter the way we feel about difficult situations and may cause an insurmountable amount of internal distress.

Another fundamental feature of DBT is *validation and acceptance* (Dimoff and Linehan 2001). The activities in this workbook are designed for you to feel validated in how you feel in your response to complex interactions. Drawing on DBT techniques of mindfulness, emotion regulation, distress tolerance, and interpersonal effectiveness, these activities will guide you toward self-acceptance and personal change (Linehan 1993; Lynch et al. 2006).

Ultimately, the activities in this book will help you find liberation from faulty ways of thinking, internal chaos, and thorny social relationships. They'll also help you reduce overall stress and boost your well-being. You can start by allowing yourself to be who you are with the understanding that you can always improve.

The structure of this book includes some warm-up chapters (1–3) to help you gain an understanding of how stress impacts your health, create a support network, and build your strengths to guide you through the DBT process.

The subsequent chapters (4–7) are designed around the therapeutic delivery of DBT and are folded into the core concepts of acceptance and change.

- **ACCEPTANCE:** mindfulness and distress tolerance

- **CHANGE:** emotion regulation and interpersonal effectiveness

We hope that your interactions with this book will help you begin to change the way you think, accept who you are, and free yourself from any negative emotions that have hindered your day-to-day life.

LETTER TO TEEN ADVOCATES

Dear Clinicians and Counselors,

Adolescent development is marked by uncertainty, tension, and adversity, leading to intense emotional stress (Florêncio, Bezerra Sousa, da Costa Silva, and Ramos 2017). Adolescents must cope with a series of developmental changes while managing challenging environmental and psychosocial stressors (Putnam 2015; Garcia 2013; Garcia et al. 2018, 2020; Collins and DeRigne 2017). In fact, adolescents are experiencing heightened levels of stressors more so than any other generation in American history (APA 2014, 2017).

This workbook is designed to help teens understand the key concepts of DBT: *mindfulness, emotion regulation, distress tolerance*, and *interpersonal effectiveness* by using everyday language that is digestible for teens to process and practice. The language shared in this book is meant to enable adolescents to find comfort in utilizing therapeutic tools to decrease daily stressors through DBT activities. This is especially important since approximately half of all adolescents in the US report a minimum of one adverse childhood experience (Child and Adolescent Health Measurement Initiative 2018–2019), which threatens mental health.

Each chapter in this workbook uniquely presents primary DBT concepts using intuitive adaptations to deliver a complex therapeutic intervention in an approachable and less intimidating manner for teens, serving as a catalyst to self-understanding and an aid to combat mental health struggles. This allows teens to use therapeutic resources to mediate stress using accessible DBT methods.

The pervasive benefits of DBT have been well documented, with clients reporting a profound shift in how they feel and improvements in everyday functioning. We recommend that a constellation of activities within the four core domains of DBT be used within your clinical sessions, as therapeutic homework between sessions, or for your teen mental health consumers to work on independently (please see Framework of DBT Activities in the appendices).

We hope this DBT workbook serves as a bridge to understand your client, build rapport, and support the assessment and case conceptualization process.

—Dr. Garcia and Wilson Ho

CHAPTER 1

STRESS IS YOUR FRENEMY

Like most teens, you're probably experiencing heightened levels of general stress due to conflicts, hardship, adversity, and expectations. In fact, teens today experience stress more than any other generation in American history. But what is stress?

Well, *stress* is your body's physical response to difficult circumstances that are hard to cope with. We understand you're living with many difficult scenarios that can cause heightened exposure to stress. In fact, most teens identify with at least one of the following areas of stress in their lives (Garcia et al. 2018).

AREA OF STRESS	STRESSOR	EXAMPLES
College-Bound Expectations	Pressures of school and grade success for future college and career	GPA, extracurriculars, test scores, college applications
School Experience	Managing multiple school-related activities and expectations	Managing sports, homework, grades, clubs, etc.
Mental Health	Significant psychological distress; crisis and risk-taking behavior	Expectations, pressures, crisis and coping skills
Friendship and Peer Dynamics	Managing interpersonal relations, social networks, andsocial norms	Social pressures, conflict, and friendship boundaries
Dating and Relationships	Experiences in romantic relationships that cause distress	Conflict, relationship awareness, personal neglect
Family Dynamics	Adherence to family expectations; managing relationships and conflicts	Pressure, family conflict, advocacy for self and others
Prejudice, Discrimination, and Teen Inequality	Unfair practices; differential treatment due to personal features	School-based and minority status discrimination
Identity Development	Internal conflict due to identity exploration	Resiliency, external biases, minority status discrimination

These stressors are known to be potential threats to your overall wellness, so it's important to understand and reflect on stressful experiences. There may be many spaces and experiences you endure that trigger your stress, and it's easy to underestimate how these stressors can impact your physical and emotional well-being—but you're not alone!

This workbook will share real-life stories from teenagers who've experienced many of the stressors you likely face. Activities in this workbook will help you to identify the stress areas listed above and provide you with strategies to manage and overcome daily stressors to improve your well-being. Handling your *emotions*, the natural feelings that affect your mood, will support your overall health. So, let's get started with reading about Theo, who is dealing with a stressor at school:

✱ THEO'S STORY

Theo is a high school senior who is trying to complete his courses in order to get admitted into college the following year. However, his school counselor forgot to give him a specific class that was necessary to graduate. Theo had to improvise and take a semester-long class crammed into one month!

❝ The thing that made it so stressful was that he did not tell me until a month before school ended, and it was a course I needed to graduate, so I had to get my sisters involved to help me to do all the work. I had to do an online course to get it all done by the end of the year to graduate. ❞

When we worry, we center our goal on finding a solution—fixing the problem! And that's exactly what Theo did. He was feeling stressed and was able to identify his problems and tackle them. Once he addressed the problem, Theo was able to experience the excitement and rewards of graduation.

FRIEND OR FOE?

Stress can be both a friend and an enemy. It can lead to positive outcomes or dramatically compromise your health. At times, stress can feel ever-present and unmanageable. It can feel overwhelming, as if it's attached to you like your shadow. It follows you around, and you can't seem to shake it. Other times, you learn how to take control of stress and use it to your advantage. In Theo's case, as a foe, his stress put him under immense pressure to accomplish a task, but as a friend, his stress motivated him to achieve his goal.

As a frenemy, stress has three distinct pathways: healthy stress, unhealthy stress, and chronic stress. Let's explore them briefly.

HEALTHY STRESS (EUSTRESS)

Healthy stress, called "eustress," is when you feel excited or experience an accomplishment. Your pulse surges with the thrill of a great outcome! Eustress is important as it keeps you engaged, active, and motivated.

Examples of eustress: your team winning a home game, saving Princess Peach from Bowser, finishing your first 5K, beating your personal record for how long you can sleep, or even asking someone to a dance.

Write an example of healthy stress you've experienced: _____

_____

_____

_____

_____

UNHEALTHY STRESS (DISTRESS)

Unhealthy stress, called "distress," wears you down and can feel jarring. You know, like when you hold onto an icon on your phone and it shakes uncontrollably? Distress can leave you feeling worried and jittery. Distress can also lead to anxiety and be harmful to your body.

Examples of distress: reading a negative post about yourself, hearing friends gossip about you, failing a class, arguing with your romantic partner, having no support from teachers in school, worrying about college.

Write an example of unhealthy stress you've experienced: _____

_____

_____

_____

_____

CHRONIC STRESS

Chronic stress is a form of unhealthy stress that is constant due to repeated stressors. Chronic stress can have a heavy impact on your body and health. It can be life-changing. Learning new skills to manage chronic stress can help you decrease the impact on your health.

Examples of chronic stress: watching family members constantly argue at home, being constantly teased or bullied at school, getting targeted on social media, not having enough money to eat daily meals.

Write an example of chronic stress you've experienced: _____

_____

_____

_____

_____

Healthy stress (eustress) keeps us alert and provides a mechanism for survival needs. Unhealthy stress (distress) can impact your daily goals, while chronic stress impacts your long-term well-being. Like everything we do in life, we need to find a healthy balance. Too much or too little of anything can hurt anybody.

Test Your Knowledge

Draw a line to match the type of stressor with its example.

Arguing with Your Sibling	Eustress
Being Harassed by a Classmate All Semester	Distress
Asking Your Crush Out on a Date	Chronic Stress

Answers:
Arguing with Your Sibling: Distress / Being Harassed...: Chronic Stress / Asking Your Crush...: Eustress

THE ROLLER STRESSOR

Life can feel like a roller coaster. You can see the ups and downs, the escalations and drops. Life can also go extremely fast, with many unexpected turns and twists.

Imagine this: As you wait in line to get on the newly built Roller Stressor, panic begins to build. You get on the roller coaster and anticipate the Drop of Doom as you click and clack your way up a steep hill. You get to the top and scream with excitement...but you have no control over where you're going! Your stomach drops with fear. Should you laugh or cry? Be excited or scared? Maybe a little bit of both?! Everything is out of your hands during this ride—at least until you reach your destination.

Now think of a time when you felt challenged by something but were excited about reaching the end. For example, preparing to take a difficult exam and being hopeful about getting a passing grade!

Go ahead and write about a time when you were stressed with excitement:

_____

_____

_____

Each experience of stress can move in many different directions, but typically include the following:

ANTICIPATION	A strong sense that something will happen or is about to take place
ESCALATION	An intense and swift rise in emotion
BUMP-IN-THE-ROAD	An obstacle that interferes with an outcome
UNEXPECTED TWIST	An event that happens suddenly without expectation
REFLECTION	A thought or consideration; a contemplation of past actions that can lead to recovery or exhaustion

Next, identify the five points of stress based on the experience you wrote about. What was the **ANTICIPATION** point in your stress moment?

_____

_____

What was the point at which **ESCALATION** occurred?

_____

_____

What was the **BUMP-IN-THE-ROAD**?

_____

_____

What was the **UNEXPECTED TWIST**?

_____

_____

Time for a **REFLECTION** now that the ride is over! Looking back, what about this stress experience do you realize now that you hadn't while in the thick of it?

_____

_____

After a thoughtful reflection, you will either experience _recovery_ (a return to balance and place for healing) or _exhaustion_ (when you are emotionally and physically depleted). More on that in the next activity.

You can find a downloadable version of the worksheet for this exercise at the website for this book: http://www.newharbinger.com/51727.

✳ ✳ ✳ _Congratulations on digging deeper into yourself through reflection! That's what this workbook is all about! The activities will guide you through the process of identifying, reflecting on, and resolving stress._

Within our bodies, we all have a nervous system that generates our fight, flight, freeze, or fawn response to difficult situations. Let's look at how your body works during intense, stressful circumstances.

- **FIGHT:** Your body is ready to have a physical interaction against the stress situation.

- **FLIGHT:** Your body wants to run away and avoid the stress situation.

- **FREEZE:** Your body is stuck during the stress situation and you are in shock.

- **FAWN:** Your body is forcing you to agree with the stress situation to manage it ASAP.

In this next activity, you will learn more about how your nervous system recovers from intense stressors.

WHEN THE RIDE IS OVER

At the very end of your Roller Stressor, when the wheels come to a screeching halt, your next stop will be either *exhaustion* or *recovery*. Take a look at the arrows. You can go either way after a deeply stressful event.

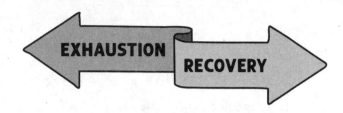

EXHAUSTION: When you're completely depleted of energy, stress has overloaded your life, and you have no more room physically or emotionally to deal with anyone or anything that challenges you. If not resolved, long-term damage to your health may be the result of exhaustion.

Think back to a time when you felt *exhausted* after a stressful event. Write about it here:

_____

_____

_____

_____

RECOVERY: A return to balance happens when your body and mind settle into a space of stability. In all the chaos, you must find your inner peace, also known as *homeostasis*. Recovering from a difficult situation will help you to build resilience to overcome future stressors.

Think back to a time when you felt yourself *recover* after a stressful event. Write about it here:

_____

_____

_____

_____

Let's apply what you learned about recovery. Write down your thoughts about the following statements to reflect on the importance of recovery.

The goal of recovery is important because	
The benefits of achieving recovery are	
Potential obstacles for recovery include	
Potential solutions for recovery include	
Specific actions to take to achieve recovery	
Any modifications needed for recovery?	

You can find a downloadable version of this worksheet for this exercise at http://www.newharbinger.com/51727.

* * * *Once you've made the active decision to choose recovery, you are building resilience. Resiliency is your "toughness," or a speedy recovery from a difficult situation. It can also mean taking back the power and control of a stressful event that has caused you to lose a part of yourself. When you are able to regain your sense of control, you will find growth waiting for you on the other side.*

MY BODY, MY STRESS

Like the anticipation of the drop in the Roller Stressor, your body gets pumped with energy and starts to tighten up to prepare for a stressful event. Your body communicates to yourself and others the impact of stress. Sometimes, you're not even aware of the stress, so your body goes on autopilot to fight the distress for you. Check out Palomita's story for an example of how stress had affected her physically and emotionally.

✳ PALOMITA'S STORY

Palomita's friends were constantly fighting and not getting along. She could never express her perspective on her friends' differences, as they simply shut her out from the friend group; they were so focused on their own anger that they didn't even notice how much it affected her. As much as she tried to resolve her friends' problems, Palomita's stress was so overwhelming that she noticed physical and emotional changes in herself. Palomita had been silenced so often that she began to feel shortness of breath and started having back pains.

> ❝ I noticed that the overwhelming stress showed through in more of a physical way. For example, by causing knots all up and down my back and my whole demeanor to change. ❞

Palomita, who was once always upbeat and positive, felt sad when she noticed her friends fighting. She felt like no one wanted to hear what she had to say, and it left her feeling abandoned. With all this pent-up energy from biting her tongue and feeling isolated, Palomita recognized that her physical and emotional stress were one and the same.

More often than not, when we are not voicing our concerns, our bodies will speak about those issues for us. It's crucial to identify how stress affects you.

Pay attention to your body right now from head to toe.

What parts of your body are screaming at you? Any physical sensations like tightening of the chest, tense shoulders, tired feet, or head feeling numb?

If yes, please describe physical symptoms:

_____

_____

_____

_____

_____

Now, pay attention to your emotions. How do you feel when you sense these symptoms?

_____

_____

_____

_____

_____

_____

Check off all the emotional and physical stress reactions you've experienced after a stressful event. You can also write in any reactions you experience that aren't on this list.

EMOTIONAL IMPACT OF STRESS	PHYSICAL IMPACT OF STRESS
☐ Worry/anxiety	☐ Headaches
☐ Irritability	☐ Body aches/tension
☐ Sadness	☐ Numbness
☐ Lack of focus	☐ Cold body parts
☐ Dissociation	☐ Fidgety/uncontrolled shakes
☐ Aggression	☐ Low energy
☐ Rumination (negative thoughts)	☐ Shortness of breath
☐ Withdrawal/isolation	☐ High pulse rate
☐ Other: _____	☐ Other: _____

Stress–Health Impact Rating Score: _____

Add up the number of stress reactions you checked off above.
Use that number to determine how stress impacts your emotional and physical health.

STRESS-HEALTH IMPACT SCORING TABLE

0–2 = No/ Low Impact	**Not too bad!** You're going through everyday stressors like anyone else. You appear to be managing stress fairly okay. But be careful—don't let the impact of stress creep up on you further.
3–6 = Moderate Impact	**Something to watch out for!** Stress is impacting your daily life activities. Making stress reduction a priority through the strategies in this book will help you get back to feeling like yourself again.
7 or more = High Impact	**Oof.** You definitely need to figure out how to manage your stress. Your health deserves some support! You can work through the impact of stress using activities in this workbook. But don't be afraid to ask someone for help. You're definitely worth it!

What are your reactions to the score that you received? Place an X on the "Impact Scale" below that best describes how you feel about your Stress-Health Impact Rating Score:

NO IMPACT   **SOMEWHAT IMPACTED**   **VERY MUCH IMPACTED**

0   1   2   3   4   5   6   7   8   9   10

Why do you think you got this score?

_____

_____

_____

_____

_____

_____

_____

_____

✳ ✳ ✳ *We can be unaware of the number of stressors we hold onto daily, both emotionally and physically. Being conscious of your stressors is critical to understanding what is causing tension in your daily life. With proper understanding, you can empower yourself to manage and cope with daily stressors.*

CHAPTER 2

MIRROR, MIRROR

SO WHERE DOES STRESS SHOW UP IN YOUR LIFE? What stressors are you experiencing? How do you typically react to stressful situations? This chapter answer helps you answer these questions by inviting you to take a look at yourself. Don't worry, you're not under a glaring spotlight of scrutiny! Rather, it's an opportunity to get to know your stress so you can get better at managing it.

Self-reflection is an art that will allow you to examine yourself more deeply. It's an opportunity to consider your behaviors, thoughts, motivations, and personal desires. More importantly, self-reflection will help you examine your responses to stressful events and circumstances that cause you pain and discomfort. Self-reflection is not always an easy practice, especially with our phones dinging, notification pop-ups, and of course, our minds swirling with the stress of our fast-paced lives. But it can provide you with the growth and understanding needed to cope with difficult situations.

Let's press pause and learn the valuable practice of self-reflection.

TRAIL TO SELF-REFLECTION

For this activity, you will want to minimize distractions. So the first thing you can do is silence your phone. Next, find a quiet space for a few moments to connect with yourself privately. Now, visualize the following scenario to practice self-reflection:

* * * *Visualizing a goal and the accompanying challenges is a form of self-reflection. Envisioning yourself winning at life can help you achieve self-growth, build personal strength, and gain a deeper understanding of yourself and who you want to be.*

MY ACCOMPLISHMENT: You made it to the top! You used every ounce of your last bit of energy and achieved your goal. The view at the top is breathtaking; the breeze cools you down. Take some time to visualize the accomplishments of your end goal. Do you see yourself getting the grade? Graduating from high school? Resolving relationship troubles?

MY STRATEGY: You're close to the peak of the mountain! You will need to muster up your full strength to keep hiking to the top. You're almost there, but how can you efficiently use your remaining strength to complete the challenge? What strategy will you use? Walking slower with more water breaks? Sprinting to the top and relaxing after you reach the peak?

MY CHALLENGE: Continuing on the trail, you look ahead and see the peak of the mountain. You decide you want to keep climbing to reach that peak. You know it might be a difficult activity, but you've decided to take on the challenge. What are your current challenges? Family conflict? Relationship troubles?

MY GOAL: You're hiking down a peaceful trail surrounded by greenery and tall trees. You feel a cool breeze and see the trees swaying to and fro while breathing in fresh air. Take a deep breath and visualize a goal you want to achieve. What is that goal? Think of something you want to achieve in your life. Getting good grades? Graduating from high school? Getting into college?

WHAT WOULD YOU DO?

Learning how to self-reflect is a technique you can use to deal with difficult circumstances. Since we know that holding up a mirror to yourself can feel a little awkward, let's practice by looking at what you might do if you were in other teenagers' shoes. The following stories illustrate common stressors in each of the eight areas of stress you learned about in chapter 1. Read the stories, then reflect and write about what you would do.

✳ ELOISE'S STORY

>❝ I experience stress mostly because I am a senior in high school and will be going to college in the fall. I have been trying to keep my high GPA and still have a social life and hang out with my friends, but it is very difficult to juggle all of that. ❞

How well do you relate to Eloise's story? Place an X in the box that best describes your relatability.

NOT RELATABLE   **SOMEWHAT RELATABLE**   **VERY MUCH RELATABLE**

0   1   2   3   4   5   6   7   8   9   10

What would be your immediate emotional response to this situation? Circle all that apply.

ANGER	ANXIETY	HOPELESSNESS	FEAR
FRUSTRATION	SADNESS	WITHDRAWAL	DISGUST
IRRITATION	WORRY	APATHY	NUMBNESS

Now, reflect on how you might address Eloise's issue. What would you do?

_____

_____

_____

_____

✳ CHARLIE'S STORY

❝ Academic stress is the worst for me, along with being self-conscious. I feel like if you're not smart or athletic then you're not doing something right. I'm scared to get a C in a class cause I know I'm just average, not important or recognized. It kinda sucks. ❞

How well do you relate to Charlie's story? Place an X in the box that best describes your relatability.

NOT RELATABLE   **SOMEWHAT RELATABLE**   **VERY MUCH RELATABLE**

0   1   2   3   4   5   6   7   8   9   10

What would be your immediate emotional response to this situation? Circle all that apply.

ANGER	ANXIETY	HOPELESSNESS	FEAR
FRUSTRATION	SADNESS	WITHDRAWAL	DISGUST
IRRITATION	WORRY	APATHY	NUMBNESS

Now, reflect on how you might address Charlie's issue. What would you do?

_____

_____

_____

_____

✱ NARISSA'S STORY

❝ Well, the type of experiences that I feel have affected me would be my image. I've always dealt with weight problems and sometimes I get so into my thoughts about how guys in school view me. I just don't have the confidence all my other friends do. I started experimenting with beer and weed. Sometimes it is peer pressure and trying to fit in, but other times it is to numb my pain and escape. I just wish I had more confidence in myself so I wouldn't put my body through the pain. ❞

How well do you relate to Narissa's story? Place an X in the box that best describes your relatability.

NOT RELATABLE					SOMEWHAT RELATABLE					VERY MUCH RELATABLE
0	1	2	3	4	5	6	7	8	9	10

What would be your immediate emotional response to this situation? Circle all that apply.

ANGER	ANXIETY	HOPELESSNESS	FEAR
FRUSTRATION	SADNESS	WITHDRAWAL	DISGUST
IRRITATION	WORRY	APATHY	NUMBNESS

Now, reflect on how you might address Narissa's issue. What would you do?

_____

_____

_____

_____

* RILEY'S STORY

66 I am not very organized with my schoolwork all the time, and I have often forgotten homework assignments given over the weekend. I will usually finish my homework in the morning before school, during classes, or during break. This doesn't allow me to spend much time with my friends, so I do not always have time to develop new relationships. 99

How well do you relate to Riley's story? Place an X in the box that best describes your relatability.

NOT RELATABLE   **SOMEWHAT RELATABLE**   **VERY MUCH RELATABLE**

0   1   2   3   4   5   6   7   8   9   10

What would be your immediate emotional response to this situation? Circle all that apply.

ANGER	ANXIETY	HOPELESSNESS	FEAR
FRUSTRATION	SADNESS	WITHDRAWAL	DISGUST
IRRITATION	WORRY	APATHY	NUMBNESS

Now, reflect on how you might address Riley's issue. What would you do?

_____

_____

_____

_____

✱ LEE'S STORY

❝ My relationship with my boyfriend wasn't stressful at first, but as time went on, it became a major stressor in my life. I guess he felt he didn't need to treat me as well as he did in the beginning. There were several incidents in which his actions made me feel terrible and insecure about myself. ❞

How well do you relate to Lee's story? Place an X in the box that best describes your relatability.

NOT RELATABLE　　　　　　　**SOMEWHAT RELATABLE**　　　　　　　**VERY MUCH RELATABLE**

0　　1　　2　　3　　4　　5　　6　　7　　8　　9　　10

What would be your immediate emotional response to this situation? Circle all that apply.

ANGER	ANXIETY	HOPELESSNESS	FEAR
FRUSTRATION	SADNESS	WITHDRAWAL	DISGUST
IRRITATION	WORRY	APATHY	NUMBNESS

Now, reflect on how you might address Lee's issue. What would you do?

_____

_____

_____

_____

_____

✱ CLEO'S STORY

❝ There was a conflict between myself, my mom, and my grandparents. My grandparents were being very verbally abusive to my mother, and it made me not want to be around them anymore. I didn't know what to do. It was like an eye opener of who they were and how they treated her and me. I think they may have treated us like that because we are different from them. ❞

How well do you relate to Cleo's story? Place an X in the box that best describes your relatability.

NOT RELATABLE   **SOMEWHAT RELATABLE**   **VERY MUCH RELATABLE**

0   1   2   3   4   5   6   7   8   9   10

What would be your immediate emotional response to this situation? Circle all that apply.

ANGER	ANXIETY	HOPELESSNESS	FEAR
FRUSTRATION	SADNESS	WITHDRAWAL	DISGUST
IRRITATION	WORRY	APATHY	NUMBNESS

Now, reflect on how you might address Cleo's issue. What would you do?

_____

_____

_____

_____

_____

✱ MARTIN'S STORY

❝ I feel like inequality and social justice is such a big issue at this school because, despite how much our school likes to call itself progressive, there are several injustices toward minority groups in general. The teachers can often contribute to this, and it becomes increasingly difficult to deal with it. ❞

How well do you relate to Martin's story? Place an X in the box that best describes your relatability.

NOT RELATABLE   **SOMEWHAT RELATABLE**   **VERY MUCH RELATABLE**

0   1   2   3   4   5   6   7   8   9   10

What would be your immediate emotional response to this situation? Circle all that apply.

ANGER	ANXIETY	HOPELESSNESS	FEAR
FRUSTRATION	SADNESS	WITHDRAWAL	DISGUST
IRRITATION	WORRY	APATHY	NUMBNESS

Now, reflect on how you might address Martin's issue. What would you do?

_____

_____

_____

_____

_____

✱ SIDNEY'S STORY

    ❝ Stress eating does not help my confidence when it comes to my body. I still always feel the need to look good or wear things that the most liked or prettiest girls are wearing. That kind of stress has given me low self-esteem and self-confidence because it sometimes makes me believe that no matter what I do, I will never be pretty enough. ❞

How well do you relate to Sidney's story? Place an X in the box that best describes your relatability.

NOT RELATABLE   **SOMEWHAT RELATABLE**   **VERY MUCH RELATABLE**

0   1   2   3   4   5   6   7   8   9   10

What would be your immediate emotional response to this situation? Circle all that apply.

ANGER	ANXIETY	HOPELESSNESS	FEAR
FRUSTRATION	SADNESS	WITHDRAWAL	DISGUST
IRRITATION	WORRY	APATHY	NUMBNESS

Now, reflect on how you might address Sidney's issue. What would you do?

_____

_____

_____

_____

✱ ✱ ✱ *You may not have control over stressful circumstances, but you do have control over what path you will take to minimize the impact of stress on your life. Reflection after a stressor is an important part of this process. Take a second to pause and think deeply about how your body and mind feel after a stressful event. This will help you to find the path to recovery rather than exhaustion.*

FROM REFLECTION TO INSIGHT

Self-reflection helps you understand how you respond to stressful situations that cause you significant distress. This is known as *self-insight*, the ability to gain a deep understanding of who you are. Building self-insight through self-reflection is like holding up a mirror to yourself. It will help you see the layers of who you are and ultimately support a strong sense of self to take on any challenge. The following exercises will help you do just that.

CLOCKING MY STRESS

Now that you've reflected on the stressors of other teenagers who are dealing with complex issues, let's dig a bit deeper into what stresses you out.

Reflect on which of the following you have had to deal with as a teenager. How much stress have each of these stressors caused you?

	NO STRESS	LOW STRESS	MODERATE STRESS	HIGH STRESS
COLLEGE-BOUND EXPECTATIONS (Ex. GPA; College Applications)	☐	☐	☐	☐
SCHOOL EXPERIENCE (Ex. Homework; Sports)	☐	☐	☐	☐
MENTAL HEALTH (Ex. Crisis; Coping Skills)	☐	☐	☐	☐
FRIENDSHIP AND PEERS (Ex. Conflicts; Boundaries)	☐	☐	☐	☐
DATING AND RELATIONSHIPS (Ex. Self-Neglect; Awareness of Others)	☐	☐	☐	☐
FAMILY DYNAMICS (Ex. Pressure; Advocacy)	☐	☐	☐	☐

	NO STRESS	LOW STRESS	MODERATE STRESS	HIGH STRESS
PREJUDICE, DISCRIMINATION & INEQUALITY (Ex. Unfair Practices Towards Teens)	☐	☐	☐	☐
IDENTITY DEVELOPMENT (Ex. Minority Status & Resilience)	☐	☐	☐	☐

(Garcia et al. 2020)

✱ ✱ ✱ *When you reflect, you're able to better understand the layers behind stressors, what caused them, and perhaps even how to solve them. Ultimately, self-reflection is a technique that will help you learn problem-solving skills, reduce your stress, and learn more about yourself.*

FACE-TO-FACE WITH MY STRESSORS

Now it's time to go face-to-face with your stressors. We know that reviewing your stress ratings can feel triggering, but it's important to reflect on stressful experiences so you can learn more about yourself and reduce the impact of stressors on your daily life. After all, what is a solution without a problem?

Create an image in your mind about one of the stressful experiences you've had. Draw it out below. It can be as real or as abstract as you'd like.

Take a look at what you drew and think about what it represents:

What was the cause of the stressor?

_____

_____

_____

Who was involved in the stressful event?

_____

_____

_____

How did this experience make you feel?

_____

_____

_____

How might you make a different decision next time?

_____

_____

_____

What might you say to yourself next time you're in this situation?

_____

_____

_____

You likely experienced a series of uncomfortable emotions when you started thinking about stressful situations. Here is your chance to reflect on the emotions that came up for you.

Circle all the emotions you experienced while self-reflecting on your stressful event:

ANGER	HOPELESSNESS	WORRY
FRUSTRATION	APATHY	DISGUST
IRRITATION	ANXIETY	NUMBNESS
FEAR	SADNESS	WITHDRAWAL

✳ ✳ ✳ *Exploring stress through self-reflection is an important tool for growth, understanding, and resiliency in handling stressful situations.*

E-MANTRAS

So what's an *e-mantra*? Simply put, it's an emotion mantra which you can say to yourself after a thoughtful reflection on a stress experience.

In the previous activity, you reflected on the difficult emotions you experienced during a stressful event. Sometimes these emotions can cause us significant distress and pain. It's important to set mantras to these emotions to minimize the impact of the stressful event. Let's set some boundaries with a few e-mantras.

ANGER: *It's okay to be angry, but I won't let it consume me.*

FRUSTRATION: *That made me so frustrated, but I will take a deep breath.*

IRRITATION: *How could someone do that? I deserve better because I'm worth it.*

FEAR: *That scared the s#$% out of me, but now that I know what it is, I won't let it bother me.*

HOPELESSNESS: *I'm not sure I can handle this, but I believe in myself and I can do it.*

APATHY: *That experience drained me, but I will do an activity in this workbook to reenergize myself.*

ANXIETY: *I'm anxious about what will happen next, but I can't control everything around me.*

SADNESS: *I'm sorrowful this happened, but I can find the good in anything.*

WORRY: *I often think about the worst-case scenario, but I know that the outcome will not be that bad.*

DISGUST: *Ewww! Did that just happen? Well, that helped me survive and feel protected.*

NUMBNESS: *I am not feeling anything at this moment, but when I do feel something, I will show it gratitude.*

WITHDRAWAL: *I might feel like shutting others out, but I know I need support from those who love me.*

Every stress event is unique. Therefore, it's important to develop your own e-mantras to help you gauge the problem and set boundaries around the difficult emotions you might experience.

Use the table below to practice writing any emotions you identified earlier in this chapter and an e-mantra to go with each emotion.

EMOTION	E-MANTRA

Nicely done! Which e-mantra did you like the best? What is it about that e-mantra that you feel so connected to?

_____

_____

_____

_____

✳ ✳ ✳ *There is power in identifying our emotions. There is power in knowing what needs are being met and what needs are unmet. By having your own unique mantra, you will have a strategy to problem-solve prior to a strong emotional reaction. All the power is in yourself.*

CHAPTER 3

YOU DON'T HAVE TO BE ALONE

Many teenagers experience difficult and complex situations as part of their daily lives. When they do, it's not uncommon to feel lonely, isolated, embarrassed, or ashamed of the circumstances that have caused the stress. We understand that it can be hard to share your stress experiences with others, and life can feel like you're the only one going through it.

We promise you, you're not alone! More than one-third of teenagers say they feel overwhelmed, sad, and tired due to daily stressors, while nearly half acknowledge they are not doing enough, or are not even sure what the heck to do to manage their stress. The activities in this chapter will help you ease into developing effective coping and stress-management skills.

"DID YOU HEAR ABOUT...?!"

Chances are, there are numerous teens who can relate to exactly what you're experiencing. The problem is, these issues aren't being talked about. When issues aren't being talked about openly, the situation can seem like it's the end of the world.

Fortunately, you can find solutions to help you live your life to your fullest potential with less stress, especially when you recognize you're not the only one going through it. Let's read some more stress narratives so you can connect with other teens like you:

✳ ROBERTO'S STORY

Roberto is a sixteen-year-old junior who is trying to juggle school, work, and his friends and family members. Like many teenagers, Roberto finds waking up at six in the morning difficult. He finds himself having to prioritize duties and tasks on a day-to-day and sometimes hour-to-hour basis! He sure is a tough one, but even the tough ones can feel overwhelmed and exhausted too.

❝ After coming from a long day of school and then going to work it often stresses me. By Friday I am usually tired but still have to go to work. When my friends invite me to hang out, I usually don't have the time, and when I do I am just too tired and would rather sleep. When I am stressed, playing video games and taking long showers help me feel better. **❞**

Can you relate to Roberto's struggle? What is your reaction to his story? Circle the emoji(s) that best describe your reaction after reading Roberto's story:

LIKE   DISLIKE   LOVE   HAHA   WOW   SAD   ANGRY

How much do you connect with this story?

_____

_____

_____

_____

✳ CAMILA'S STORY

Camila just graduated from high school and received pressure from her family members to either continue with school or get a job. She decided to attend culinary school, but it was much more like work than school.. It all felt like foreign territory. Adulting was hard! Camila's family had high expectations for her to be accomplished and successful, but with all the pressures of success starting to seep in, she felt ready to quit.

❝ There have been times where I just want to drop out, but I can't find it in me to actually tell my parents that I can't take the stress. I also do not want to let my family down like my older sister, who dropped out of the university when she became pregnant. I also have a brother that graduated from high school last year and isn't doing anything to better himself. **❞**

Despite Camila feeling like she had the weight of the world on her, she persisted and motivated herself by wanting to be better.

> I have told myself that I can't be like them, but it is a lot of pressure. If I quit now, I will only be another disappointment. It's been hard these past couple of months going from being a kid to becoming an adult. But I do know that I can overcome it, and I know I have to try to stay positive.

It can't be easy to have everyone relying on you to be the pride and joy of the family. But nonetheless, Camila realized that she still wants to live up to everyone's expectations of her, and that is what motivates her the most. With all this trust that the family has placed on Camila, she comes to realize that she is trusted for a reason—to overcome obstacles and transform from a teenager into an adult.

Can you relate to Camila's struggle? What is your reaction to her story? Circle the emoji(s) that best describe your reaction after reading Camila's story:

LIKE   DISLIKE   LOVE   HAHA   WOW   SAD   ANGRY

How much do you connect with this story?

_____

_____

_____

✳ EREN'S STORY

Like most teens, Eren is having difficulty managing multiple responsibilities in his daily life. As a high-school junior, Eren experiences a lot of pressure to be involved in extracurriculars, as well as maintain an above-average GPA to finish high school and get into college. We all know how hard that can be, especially when it interferes with well-being... Eren is sleep deprived and finds himself unable to keep up with all the homework that is assigned to him.

❝ Sometimes I don't end up doing all my homework, and then my grades will go down, and that is what stresses me out the most. I also get stressed out when I don't have time to study for tests or finals that really impact my grade. It bothers me so much that my GPA should be higher, and I can't do much about it because I need sleep and time to complete my work, not to mention I do sports, and that takes up my time too, and it can get pretty hard to keep up with my classes. ❞

It seems that teenagers need to be extraordinary these days. Like with Eren, he needs energy to do well in sports, which compromises the energy he needs to do schoolwork. Eren is caught having to find a balance with the limited time that is given to everyone in a day. It can present quite a challenge to Eren and many other teenagers.

Can you relate to Eren's struggle? What is your reaction to his story? Circle the emoji(s) that best describe your reaction after reading Eren's story:

LIKE   **DISLIKE**   **LOVE**   **HAHA**   **WOW**   **SAD**   **ANGRY**

How much do you connect with this story?

_____

_____

_____

_____

✳ ✳ ✳ *Realizing you're not alone through these stories is an important part of your process to connect with other teens. Teens of all ages experience similar stressors, but your stories are not shared nearly enough. When teens aren't sharing their stress experiences, they can feel isolated, lonely, and confused. This can lead to depression, anxiety, substance use, and suicide. But you really aren't alone! The more you share, the more you connect, and the unity in the voices of you and other teens can create meaningful change in how you perceive those experiences.*

THE STRUGGLE IS REAL

Now is your chance to tell your story! Review the eight areas of stress below (see chapter 1 for stressor examples if you need a refresher) and consider what category, or categories, of stress you've experienced. Circle any and all stress areas that have caused you a heightened amount of difficulty.

College-Bound Expectations

School Experience

Mental Health

Friendship and Peer Dynamics

Dating and Relationships

Family Dynamics

Prejudice, Discrimination, and Teen Inequality

Identity Development

It's true, life is stressful! But the good news is that you can reduce your stress. You can start by thinking for a moment about one or more of the stress areas you just circled that was quite difficult for you. When you're ready, write your stress story on the following page:

Go ahead and reread the story you just wrote. This will help you to understand the type of stress you've experienced. Now, let's see how your stressors connect with other teens who have also shared difficult times. Again, we promise, you're not alone!

DO YOU RELATE?

Let's see how well you relate to other teens. Do you feel like any of their examples hit home for you? If so, explain why in the space provided.

AREA OF STRESS	STORY	DO YOU RELATE? (Y/N/WHY?)
Prejudice, Discrimination, Inequality	I struggle a lot in school. Usually when I ask for help, teachers just say it's because I'm not focused, which is false. I study often and always ask for help.	
Identity	Something that gives me exponential stress is the need to fit in. I find myself looking to others to see how I should act, or what I should do or say.	
School Experience	My future depends on how I do in school, and I feel that school causes so much stress to the point where we can't enjoy our lives.	
Family Dynamics	I'm afraid that if I don't apply and get into the schools that my father wants, it will cause a huge fight between my parents.	

AREA OF STRESS	STORY	DO YOU RELATE? (Y/N/WHY?)
Dating and Relationships	The stress of being in a relationship that is not healthy but you don't want to give up and have to start again...having a kid at a young age is stressful as well because you have to balance your life with school and having a family.	
Mental Health	When I was sixteen, my dad passed away. I have my good days and I have my bad days. I still cry almost every day, due to the fact that I miss him a lot. I try to make him proud, but sometimes it's just so hard.	
Friendship and Peer Dynamics	When I was in middle school, I was often bullied by other kids because I had acne. It affected me a lot because for a while, I wouldn't wanna leave the house without putting makeup on. Even when all my face got cleared up, I was still not comfortable. It changed how I felt about myself for a while.	

You can find a downloadable version of the worksheet for this exercise at http://www.newharbinger.com/51727.

EASE INTO IT

Along with our colleagues, we have created the Everyday Adolescent Stress Experiences (EASE) scale to help teens assess and rate their level of stress. This online activity will help you to reflect on your stressors in a concrete way. When you get your results, you'll be able to construct goals within this workbook to reduce your stress.

To better understand your stressors, use the QR code to take the EASE test:

After completing the EASE scale online (anonymously of course!), you will receive results of each subscale and your overall stress ratings. These scores will help you better understand what distressing situations are most likely to impact you.

Go ahead and transfer your EASE stress scores into the boxes below:

College-Bound Expectations:

School Experience:

Mental Health:

Friendship and Peer Dynamics:

Dating and Relationships:

Family Dynamics:

Prejudice, Discrimination, and Inequality:

Identity Development:

Overall EASE Stress Score:

Review your EASE results and reflect upon them by completing the statement below:

The stress areas I received the highest ratings in are:

_____

_____

_____

Well, I'm not surprised! I understand I got these results because:

_____

_____

_____

Now that I know my stressors more clearly, what am I willing to do about them?

_____

_____

_____

Hey wait, I'm not alone! I know some other people (perhaps teens whose stories are told in this workbook) who have had similar stress experiences to mine. They are:

_____

_____

_____

Maybe sharing my stress results with someone else won't be that bad. But before I share my stress experiences, maybe I should check on my comfort level.

Shade in your comfort level for sharing your stress experiences and EASE results with the person or people you identified above:

HMMM ... NOT QUITE COMFY　　　　　　　　**SOMEWHAT COMFY**　　　　　　　　**VERY MUCH COMFY**

0　　1　　2　　3　　4　　5　　6　　7　　8　　9　　10

Now that you know your comfort level for sharing, who might be the best person with whom you'd like to share your experiences? You may want to consider someone who has had similar life experiences. Remember, you don't have to be alone, yet we also want to emphasize that there is no obligation to share. If you do, it's best done with a trusted person or group.

The people I feel comfortable sharing my stress story and stress ratings with:

1. _____

2. _____

3. _____

✳ ✳ ✳ *We know that sharing your personal stress experiences with others can be difficult. But when you do, you will feel empowered by using your voice to express yourself. Talking about the true essence of yourself authenticates who you are. Being open and transparent can lead to support, guidance, and advocacy for yourself and others.*

PUZZLE ME THIS!

You've spent a lot of time thinking about how your stress experiences are like those of other teens. Now it's time to put the pieces of your support puzzle together. Because remember, you don't have to be alone. So, who is the main centerpiece gluing everyone together? Who is always around? Where do you fit in the puzzle of your life?

Your puzzle support networks represent family, friends, and role models. To complete each puzzle below, find the piece that represents you and fill in your name. Then, fill in the names of people who support you.

FAMILY PUZZLE

FRIEND PUZZLE

ROLE MODEL PUZZLE

43

Your puzzles affirm that you have at least one other person in your life that can be a part of your support network. We understand that they may not always understand you or know how to talk to you about your stressful experiences. Regardless, it's good to know that there are people around you who care for you deeply and want to be a part of your life puzzle.

* * * *Magnificent! Give yourself another round of applause. One clap for getting through this chapter, one clap for continuing this workbook, and another clap for finding your support network.*

CHAPTER 4

MINDFULNESS

Mindfulness is a conscious state of mind where your sense of awareness is focused on the present moment. During this time of awareness, you are encouraged to acknowledge, accept, and interpret your feelings, sensations, and thoughts. Through the process of mindfulness techniques, you can learn how to cope with your emotions without judging yourself or others.

The benefits of mindfulness include feeling restored, empowered, and recognizing what you can and cannot control. Mindfulness will teach you how to stay in tune with the present as opposed to jumping back and forth from thoughts about the past or worries about the future.

The four components of mindfulness that you will learn through the activities in this chapter are:

1. Mindful Awareness
2. Mind–Body Connection
3. Balance and Stability
4. Self-Empowerment

The valuable techniques of mindfulness will help you build a sense of calm within your body to nurture the ultimate goal of humanity: love. Most important, love for yourself and all things around you.

MINDFUL AWARENESS

Sometimes you might be moving too fast in life, darting here and there. When this happens, you don't pay attention to your internal states and can easily forget to cherish yourself in the present. The lack of emotional and situational awareness can create internal distress without you even knowing it. So, let's do a quick activity to get a baseline of how slow or fast your life is.

Speed Check

Shade in the baseline scale to identify your pace in life.

SLOW					EHHH				FAST
0	10	20	30	40	50	60	70	80	90	100

Now that you've identified how fast-paced your life is at the present, it's important to acknowledge that it could be interfering with your internal states of awareness. Mindfulness techniques will allow you to experience life right here, right now, while in a state of peace. For example, imagine yourself floating in water where everything around you seems to have disappeared. Having that peaceful moment of serenity to just exist, as opposed to worrying about what will happen next, is what *mindful awareness* will help you to achieve.

When you try to control every aspect of every problem without being mindfully aware of your internal emotional state, there could be repercussions of intense distress—let's take a look at this next story as an example.

✴ GIA'S STORY

Gia comes from a large, chaotic family with constant tension and conflict. Her family members had difficulty communicating in a manner that was respectful and supportive. Every discussion seemed to turn into a screaming match, and sometimes this left Gia feeling too overwhelmed to even cry. The frequent family escalations Gia witnessed caused significant disruption, interfering with daily tasks.

> No one in the house was getting along, and it led me to lose focus on my academics because of all the yelling and arguments. My train of thought was focused on how to get my family back to "normal."

Every time Gia would try to redirect herself to her academic tasks, her attention would become blurred, and she struggled to ground herself.

You can see how Gia's family members were not considerate of her and how that has taken an emotional toll on Gia. Gia was so focused on problem-solving for her family that she forgot to be mindful of her own well-being. She was losing focus on her schoolwork and trapped with emotions like sadness, sorrow, anger, and resentment toward her family since she was unable to be mindful and take care of her own needs.

Sound Check: Testing...1...2...3...

It's easy to feel a lot of different emotions when you're not in the present. Being mindful includes being aware of how you're feeling, particularly during intensely stressful situations.

Check off all that apply when you're not mindfully aware:

- ☐ Rumination—stuck in constant circling thoughts

- ☐ Distracted and not focused

- ☐ Stumbling through the routine of life

- ☐ Losing sense of your connection to your self

- ☐ Losing importance and value

- ☐ Mind cloudiness or brain fog

- ☐ Anxiety and stress

- ☐ Impulsive and risk-taking behaviors

- ☐ Losing control of emotions

- ☐ Uncontrollable reactions

Of the items you checked off above, which two would you like to improve?

1. _____

2. _____

Can you write about a time when these reactions affected your *emotional state*?

_____

_____

_____

Can you write about a time when these reactions affected your *productivity levels*?

_____

_____

_____

Can you write about a time when these reactions affected your *social interactions*?

_____

_____

_____

How can changing these reactions improve your overall well-being in one or all of the areas you just wrote about?

_____

_____

_____

✳ ✳ ✳ *Noticing how you're feeling and reacting to stress is really only possible if you're in a mindful state. With practice, you can learn to be mindful of your thoughts, your emotions, and your reactions. Good news! Mindfulness activities can be quick grounding exercises that take anywhere from three to fifteen minutes with practice.*

Mini-Mindfulness Scale

How often do you think you're not grounded and connected in a mindful state? How often do you feel imbalanced and out of control? Complete the Mini-Mindfulness Scale to learn more about yourself. Rate yourself on a scale of 1 (Strongly Disagree) to 5 (Strongly Agree).

	STRONGLY DISAGREE	SOMEWHAT DISAGREE	NEITHER AGREE NOR DISAGREE	SOMEWHAT AGREE	STRONGLY AGREE
I am not always aware of my emotions.	☐	☐	☐	☐	☐
I find myself losing focus on what's happening around me.	☐	☐	☐	☐	☐
I don't feel the stress in my body until the discomfort is unbearable.	☐	☐	☐	☐	☐
I tend not to pay attention to my everyday actions.	☐	☐	☐	☐	☐
Sometimes I suddenly forget what I'm supposed to be doing.	☐	☐	☐	☐	☐

Developed by D. Garcia and W. Ho, Cal State University, Los Angeles, 2022.

Now, add up your scores for each statement using the scale below.

Strongly Disagree	1
Somewhat Disagree	2
Neither Agree nor Disagree	3
Somewhat Agree	4
Strongly Agree	5

Mindfulness Score: _____

MINDFULNESS RUBRIC:

5–11 = Very Mindful • 12–17 = Moderately Mindful • 18–25 = Unmindful

The lower your score, the more mindful you are in your everyday life. Higher scores mean less mindfulness.

Now that you know your Mindfulness Score, let's reflect.

Are you surprised about your Mindfulness Score? Why or why not?

_____

_____

_____

Check off the statement(s) in the Mini-Mindfulness Scale that you would like to improve on:

☐ I am not always aware of my emotions.

☐ I find myself losing focus on what's happening around me.

☐ I don't feel the stress in my body until the discomfort is unbearable.

☐ I tend to not pay attention when engaged in tasks.

☐ I find myself moving aimlessly and forgetting my intentions.

Why are these areas important for you to improve on?

_____

_____

_____

How would you improve yourself in those areas?

_____

_____

I'm Out of My Mind!

When you're *not* in a state of mindful awareness, you're not paying attention, which means you might say or do something you regret. Check Yes or No:

Have you ever said something to a friend that you didn't mean?

☐ Yes ☐ No

Have you ever done something impulsively?

☐ Yes ☐ No

Was it something you never thought you would do until after you actually did it?

☐ Yes ☐ No

Do you still think about it?

☐ Yes ☐ No

Does it still affect you?

☐ Yes ☐ No

It's important to reflect on these experiences, so jot down how you felt at that time:

_____

_____

_____

_____

It can feel quite unimaginable now, but it probably felt like a big deal back then. We all have moments when we really aren't ourselves and lose our sense of self-control. And that's okay!

Let's practice new versions of ourselves through mindfulness. You've snapped your fingers and you've become innately more aware of your past self. If you could redo those previous experiences...

What would you do differently?

_____

_____

_____

_____

_____

Why would you do it differently?

_____

_____

_____

How might that change the other person's reaction?

_____

_____

_____

What would you hope to accomplish?

_____

_____

_____

_____

* * * _When not in a state of mindfulness, stressful situations can feel unbearable and all consuming. It's important to recognize when you are out of balance and in a state of internal confusion. Identifying a state of instability will help you to know why you're doing what you're doing. Then you can pay attention to any reactions you may have and put in place strategies to correct them._

MIND–BODY CONNECTION

Remember in PE when your teacher would give you that awful assignment of running laps? Your leg muscles would burn from running, especially if you fixated on the leg pain instead of your breathing. Your mind is no different! Your mind can be just as tired and tense as your body when faced with a stressful situation. This is called the _Mind-Body Connection._

The mind and body coexist. So, when you fixate on your legs being sore, your mind can share the same experience, namely emotional soreness, which may lead to more bodily soreness. These fixations remove you from that internal state of peace and calm that mindfulness brings.

Connecting with yourself in a mindful state is also about identifying your bodily sensations. It's important to recognize your body's response and how it reacts when intense events happen. In fact, the only times you might recognize when something is off-balance and causing distress is when your body tells you.

Tree Visualization

Consider the book you're holding in your hands right now. Feel the smooth coolness of the book cover. Smell the pages and feel the wind as you flip through this book.

Where did this book come from? Why, trees of course! Now imagine in your mind a specific tree standing tall in a forest that made this page. Take a deep breath, and calmly and carefully consider everything you can imagine about this tree:

What does the tree look like?

_____

_____

_____

How does it feel to touch the tree?

_____

_____

What does the tree smell like?

_____

_____

How long did it take the tree to grow?

_____

_____

How much water did the tree drink from the rain?

_____

_____

See yourself standing next to the tree, getting wet from the rain. How does the water feel on your skin?

_____

_____

Reel yourself back into your present self and think about your current physical state. Connect with your body for a moment, and circle all the sensations you felt while going through the visualization activity.

SENSATIONS

TINGLY	RELAXED	GOOSEBUMPS	ACHEY
WARM	TICKLY	BUTTERFLIES	FATIGUED
FLUSTERED	TREMBLY	CALM	LIGHT IN BODY

What's the strongest sensation you felt?

_____

_____

How did that sensation support the connection between your mind and body?

_____

_____

_____

_____

* * * _Having a peaceful moment with a guided visualization and mindfulness activity will support your connection to your mind and body._

STRESSOR CIRCLES

Consider an upcoming tennis match. What part of the tennis match is strictly for the mind to stress about? What parts of the match stress the body out? What parts can affect both the mind and body? For example, your mind could be stressed about your technique and strategy. Your body could be stressed from elbow and knee pains. And both your mind and body together could be stressed for your overall performance in the match.

Can you think of more examples of the mind-body stress connection? Consider a difficult homework assignment. Write a Mind Stressor you might experience for that assignment in the Mind Circle and a Body Stressor you might experience for that assignment in the Body Circle.

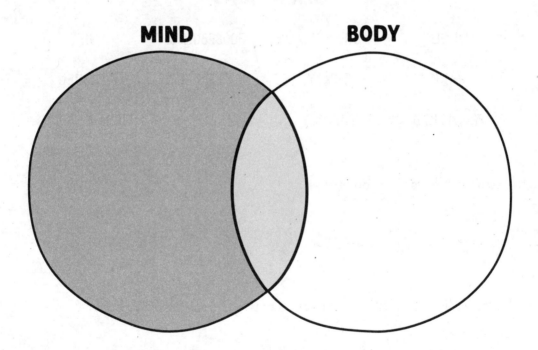

✳ GIBBS' STORY

As an only child, Gibbs felt responsible for everyone and everything. He had a lot on his plate trying to manage his schoolwork while playing sports and dealing with family issues.

❝❝ It was hard to maintain a high GPA as well as playing high school sports, volunteering at hospital and church, playing club soccer, and taking care of a sick grandma. I had to manage my time and set my priorities. ❞❞

As Gibbs was moving from one activity to the next, he was not taking the time to breathe and transition. When he finally had a moment to himself, he would feel the full effects of muscle fatigue, such as knees collapsing, back aching, shoulders tightening, and exhaustion. Although most of these side effects seem to be physical, the mental stress that started it all had finally caught up with Gibbs and forced him to break down.

Poor Gibbs... It is so difficult to recognize the synergy that comes from the mind-body connection. Often when people think about the mind and the body, they are seen as two very distinct entities. However, both parts work hand in hand with one another, and when one is underserved, the whole person suffers. Check out this next activity to better equip yourself to take care of both your *mind* and your *body*.

Embodied Stress

When your mind is swirling in a state of stress, so is your body. The Mind-Body Connection is a deeply rooted system. Paying attention to how your body reacts to stress is a form of mindfulness. To do so:

Find a quiet space.

Sit in a comfortable position.

Relax your body.

Close your eyes or find a meaningful object to focus on.

Scan your body for tension or stress.

Where do you hold your stress in your body? Did you find it?

_____

_____

_____

_____

Checklist for body-part sensations: ☐ Head ☐ Torso ☐ Lower body

Grab a pen and mark all the spots on your body where you found stress.

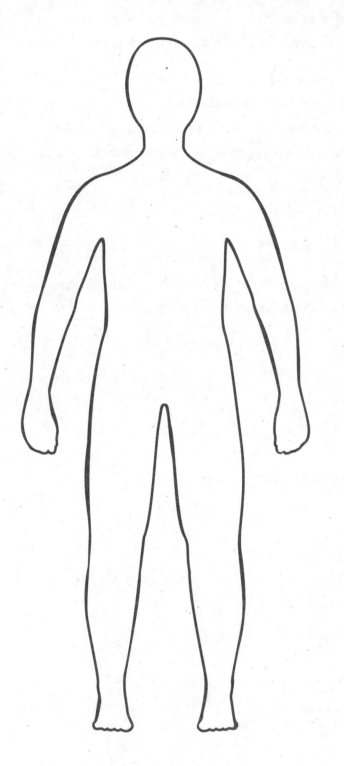

Your body holds your stress in several places. Check the specific areas in your body from the list below.

HEAD

JAW

EYES

NECK

THOAT

TORSO

SHOULDERS

STOMACH

ARMS & HANDS

CHEST

LOWER BODY

LOWER BACK

CALVES

THIGHS

FEET

Hug Life

No, we aren't going to ask you to hug yourself...well, maybe kinda. First, find a sitting position that works best for you. Close your eyes if you feel comfortable, or lower your eyelids as if you were pretending you are asleep. Next, take in some deep breaths and sit up straight. Now that you're in a comfortable position, you can do a couple of the following body hugs to release stress that's being held captive within your physical self.

SHOULDER HUG

Cross your arms and place your hands on the top-back portion of your shoulders. As you hold your shoulders, pull your stomach inward to feel a stretch in your upper back while slowly breathing in and out. Inhale for five seconds and exhale for seven seconds. The back is an area that holds a lot of stress. Let it go by breathing it out with a warm hug stretch.

VAGUS NERVE

Place your left hand on your stomach and place your right hand over your heart. Take deep breaths into your stomach, as if you are pushing out your abdomen and expanding your ribs. Inhale for five seconds and exhale for seven seconds. The longer you can exhale, the more effective the breathing becomes. If comfortable, activate your vocal cords by humming to help stimulate the vagus nerve. This technique helps to alleviate stress and pain held in the body.

BODY SCAN

Pause and scan for body parts that may need more attention and comfort. A body scan is a method used to start a mindfulness or meditation practice. Focus on the stress you find and talk to that body part as if it were one of your friends. Apply gentle pressure to those parts of your body to acknowledge where you hold your stress. We know this may feel a little silly, but this is your mind and body rekindling their relationship.

✱ ✱ ✱ *Consider using these mindfulness activities when you start to feel ramped up after a difficult day. Instead of letting your mind, emotions, and body zigzag back and forth as in a tennis match, find some time to ground yourself with these activities.*

✳ VINCENT'S STORY

Vincent's family has great expectations for him to live up to. He feels as though he's the odd one out. Most folks in his family went to Ivy League schools, and his parents expect the same of him. He feels like he can't let them down. There is a lot of pressure on him to succeed, so much so that it is starting to take a physical and mental toll.

❝ School is hard. The pressure that the school in general puts on us about college makes me feel like I'm not doing good enough. School stresses me out to the point where I don't even want to get out of bed sometimes. I'm both mentally and physically exhausted. I feel irritated, tired, or sad a lot of the time. And I feel tired no matter how much I sleep. Or sometimes I'm so anxious—tense, with my heart racing or my stomach hurting—that I can't concentrate. ❞

It's clear that a lot of Vincent's stress is manifesting in his body and mind. And it's making it even harder for him to deal with the source of his stress—school and his family's expectations. When Vincent could no longer deal with his external stressors, they impacted his physical and mental health.

5-5-5 Breathing Exercise

In this next activity, you will equip yourself with a tool to help reduce physical reactions to stress by regaining control of your body.

Let's begin this breathing activity with a few notes:

* Find a comfortable space and position to sit in.

* The outdoors is always a good option!

* You can keep your eyes open or close them.

This breathing exercise, called "5-5-5 breathing," will be based on three five-second mini-sessions of 1) Inhale, 2) Exhale, and 3) Pause-Reflect.

Think of a positive emotion you want to bring, or inhale, into your body. Now, think of a negative emotion you want to release, or exhale, from your body. Write them down here:

Positive Emotion: _____

Negative Emotion: _____

1. Now, take a deep breath in very slowly through your nose for 5 seconds and inhale that positive emotion you wrote down. Happiness? Joy? Calm?

2. Exhale the negative emotion you picked, very slowly, through your nose or mouth for five seconds. Kick that negative emotion out of your body! Goodbye anger! So long frustration!

3. Pause for five seconds to reflect on how your body feels. Relaxed? Relieved? Tense?

Repeat the process five more times, breathing in a positive emotion for 5 seconds, breathing out a negative emotion for 5 seconds, and then holding your breath for 5 seconds while you scan your body. Total breathing time is about two minutes.

✳ ✳ ✳ *How's that for Mind-Body Connection? We get so caught up with our day-to-day lives that sometimes we forget how much pressure we place on our bodies. But that's what this book is about, right? Helping you nurture both aspects so that your mind and body can thank you after!*

BALANCE AND STABILITY

Think back to your stress-inducing tennis match. Game point! You're in the middle of a rally, and the tennis ball is pinging back and forth across the net. When you are not focused and just paying attention to your opponent's moves, you may distract yourself, fall off-balance, crash to the ground, and sprain your ankle.

Finding a sense of balance and stability through mindfulness will help you unblur the dizziness that comes with your daily stressors. Keeping your emotional states in balance will help you to feel grounded, find patience, and calmly approach stressful situations with solutions (and not sprain an ankle!).

Let's work through some mindfulness activities that will help guide you through what it means to stay in the present and find stability in a world of instability. Obtain balance to collect your thoughts, maintain control of your emotions, and feel a connection to yourself.

✳ RUBY'S STORY

Ruby finally felt ready to take the next step with her boyfriend, and things got a little too intimate for school grounds. When they got caught, her teacher was in shock and went straight to the principal. Her school suspended her for a whole month.

❝ Rumors started going around, and I was too humiliated to attend my sibling's graduation. The hardest part was going back to school for the first time after getting suspended. I was worried about what people thought about me. ❞

When she walked through the hallways of her school, all she could feel were judgmental eyes and speculation. Frantic and frazzled, Ruby was doing her best to look past this event.

It was difficult for Ruby to cope because the rumor was beyond her control. Ruby was struggling with understanding how her situation got so escalated. She was stuck, not knowing how to find a solution, and her mind was short-circuiting. She lost all sense of personal balance and emotional stability.

By recognizing that everyone makes mistakes, Ruby was able to ground her thoughts and lessen her reactions to the rumors being spread about her. This in turn helped her find stability within a space of social instability.

Write about a time when you made a mistake and all eyes were on you.

_____

_____

_____

_____

_____

_____

Did you feel out of control?

☐ Yes ☐ No

Did you ignore the problem and wait for it to go away?

☐ Yes ☐ No

At some point, were you able to regain control and balance?

☐ Yes ☐ No

What did you do (if anything) to regain control and balance after making a mistake?

_____

_____

_____

_____

_____

_____

_____

_____

✳ ✳ ✳ *If you haven't figured out how to recover from mistakes, that's okay! It takes a lot of emotional energy to own and correct them. All humans (especially adults) are a work in progress. When a mistake occurs, it's important to balance yourself with mindfulness activities to help you find solutions.*

THINK ABOUT IT

Let's say your science presentation is due tomorrow but the basketball tournament is this weekend! And you need to perform a song in a play that same day! How do you juggle it all?! You'd likely feel overwhelmed, of course, which can set off a chain reaction of fear, anxiety, and stress. Before that happens, use these activities to calmly manage all you have going on and find stability to get it done.

PETx Talk!

Take a moment to think about your pet, if you have one (if you don't have a pet, that's okay— just think of your ideal pet). Often, having a pet is great. But when you're meeting a new pet for the first time, even if it's your ideal pet, it'll probably stress you out! You have to get to know your pet before you can have a good relationship with it.

It's the same with your stress! You'll need to connect with your stress to understand how it affects you and to learn how to tame your stress, just like your new pet. Take a moment and draw your imaginary "stress pet" in the box.

- What color is it?

- Is it a blob or symmetrical?

- Is it a scribble? Fine lines?

- Is it big or small?

- Draw yourself along with your *stress pet* as a size comparison.

  * Is it looming over you?

  * Is it next to you?

  * Is it hiding behind you?

As a new pet owner, you'll also need to learn how to communicate with and train your pet. So when your new, ideal pet starts to overwhelm you (someone had an accident!), you'll want to gently walk it back to its habitat until you are ready to be with it.

You'll need to do the same when you're overwhelmed with stress. Sometimes, you'll need to gently set your stress aside and put it on a time-out until you're in a better space to handle it. It's important to uncover your stress...but at a pace that feels right for you, or it will be too hard to find your balance.

When you're ready to face your stress, you'll want to ask yourself some questions and describe your answers below:

Why did this stress me out?

_____

_____

_____

Why did I get so overwhelmed?

_____

_____

_____

Where did this stress come from?

_____

_____

What was the trigger for my stress?

_____

_____

With the stress you just considered, go back to your drawing and shade in your stress pet with the color you associate your stress with, e.g., anger = red, sadness = blue.

What color did you use?

_____

_____

What type of stress does this color represent?

_____

_____

Stress Pet

Your stress pet is a good metaphor for the real stress you encounter. Sometimes our pets can be excited and jump all over us, and maybe even have a little accident (oops!). Sometimes, they approach with caution. Here is an example of how stress can manifest:

Dr. Garcia has a dog named Minnie that is involved in daily shenanigans. While Dr. Garcia visited a family member at a hospital, Minnie escaped from the car and dashed into the hospital. Minnie ran through the lobby, turned down a hall, and made her way to the patient lunchroom. In this story, we can see that Minnie was 1) troublesome, 2) causing an immense amount of stress to Dr. Garcia as she chased her down the hallway, and 3) relieving her own stress. Yes! Minnie was simply trying to find a way to relieve her own stress! She was hungry and was trying to find food, and once she did, she stopped.

Although stress can bring up such headaches, it also serves a purpose. Think of a time when your stress disrupted your life. When your stress pet comes at you, you'll need to slowly get acquainted with it so that it doesn't spin out of control.

When you first become aware of your stress pet, you'll probably want to do the following:

- Let your stress pet carefully sniff at your fingers (no biting!)

- Rather than pulling away from your stress pet, think, *why is it sniffing?*

  * To get more acquainted with you?

  * To check out what you ate for lunch?

  * To feel more connected with you?

Here are a couple of ways your stress pet can help you reduce your stress:

- Talk to your stress pet to alleviate stress.

- Go on a walk with your stress pet.

- Hold your stress pet and soothe it with a cuddle.

- Perhaps, laugh with your stress pet.

* * * *Great work reflecting on your stressors and getting acquainted with them. We know that some stressful situations cause uncertainty and you have no control over them. You will likely feel overwhelmed, stressed, and even defeated. But there are ways to cope if you know how to ground yourself.*

* SESA-ME'S STORY

Sesa-Me volunteered to share their story about overthinking. Instead of overanalyzing and getting caught up in the future, they grounded themselves in the present.

Sesa-Me comes from an accomplished family and does not want to let them down. Their whole life they had dreamed of being a lawyer, and they strive to be a perfectionist. Although they are hyper-focused on achieving their goals, they recognize they're giving up their youth.

> **❝** I would like to be the best I can in school, and my parents expect the same of me. My future depends on how I do in school, and I feel that school causes so much stress to the point where we can't enjoy our young teen lives. **❞**

Sesa-Me was able to reflect on their stress and understand its impact. Let's practice how to look at your surroundings to paint a picture of your stress. Pausing to reflect on your stress will help you to move toward homeostasis—a state of emotional stability.

Take A Look

Let's take that pause and do some reflecting in this section.

Take a moment to look at the room you're in right now.

Visually scan up, down, and around the room.

Pay attention to the walls, furniture, and items in the room (pictures, bedding, collectibles).

How big is your window? What do you see outside?

_____

_____

_____

_____

_____

What things in this room make you feel anxious?

_____

_____

_____

_____

Now that you've identified the item that makes you feel anxious, remove it from sight, if you can. Doing so helps to create a neutral space that makes you feel comfortable and settled, especially when you're starting to feel a bit out of control.

Let's do another scan of the room:

Visually scan up, down, and around the room again.

Pay attention to any items that bring you comfort.

What things in this room make you feel comfortable?

_____

_____

_____

Once you find an object that makes you feel comfortable, take hold of the object and inspect it. Observe. Ask yourself why it makes you feel a sense of comfort and calm.

Is it the touch? What does it feel like?

_____

_____

_____

_____

Is it the smell? What does it smell like?

_____

_____

_____

_____

Is it a memory tied to the object? When seeing this object, what is the first memory you think of?

_____

_____

_____

Once you are able to recognize the sense of comfort the item brings, honor it by thanking the object or hugging the object. It's important to acknowledge the items that bring you comfort, particularly if they hold a special memory that brings you joy and a moment of stability.

* * * *Snap a picture of the comfort object and refer to the picture when you feel like you need something to ground you. Grounding activities are ultimately meant to help you find equilibrium when your stress is heightened.*

* ASHTON'S STORY

Ashton had a load of stressors that he really didn't know how to manage. He struggled with feeling lonely and not good enough for anyone. He always felt like his peers were criticizing him and shutting him out of the group. To gain their approval, he would act out or buy things that were expensive and superficial, even if he didn't like them.

> 66 They were very judgmental of me and would critique anything about me—from my shoes to my personality to my phone or even my laugh. I was not really being who I wanted to be, but who my peers wanted. 99

Not having a sense of belonging and concentrating on others' perceptions of him, Ashton didn't feel like himself. If you can relate to this scenario, the next mindfulness activity will help ground you back to personal stability during a moment when you feel less confident.

Comfort Object

A comfort object is something you can grab onto during overwhelming and stressful situations to calm your mind and bring you back to emotional homeostasis. Typically, this could be an animal, a blanket, or even a person close to you.

First, identify a comfort object that most appeals to you and take some time to draw it below. If you can, choose a different object than the one you picked in the previous activity.

Where did you get this object, and why is it important?

_____

_____

_____

Why does it provide comfort?

_____

_____

Hold your comfort object close. What does it smell like?

_____

_____

Does the smell of the object remind you of someone or something important to you?

_____

_____

What memories does it evoke as you're holding onto it?

_____

_____

Turning from what is troubling you and toward an everyday comfort object can help you to regain power over intense and unfamiliar situations, which you can't always control.

✳ ✳ ✳ *When you're in the middle of a stressful crisis, you will likely feel out of control. Identifying and tracking where it comes from will guide you toward solutions so that you can regain control of yourself. Your comfort object can help you gain a sense of power over your stressful situation.*

SELF-EMPOWERMENT

An important result of mindfulness training and techniques is the ability to gain a sense of self-empowerment. Through the following activities, you will be able to take action for yourself, regain control of your emotions, and forge your own destiny by using your voice to make the best decisions for yourself.

✳ DOUG'S STORY

Doug is an aspiring actor and gets critiqued every day on the stage. He is very critical of himself, and his biggest fear is failing. Any time he senses an imperfection, his body begins to panic. He loses his sense of self-control until he is able to label his stressors.

> ❝ I am aware that it is not a good trait to have because I know I cannot be perfect and will never be, but it is something that is always in my mind. If something slightly goes wrong, I freak out. I am often in a constant state of anxiety and stress that I find difficult to shake off. ❞

Doug found he can recognize the situations that are a crisis for him—like when he notices he's messed up a line or sees a frown on the director's face. And while his stress is often high, Doug notices when and why it spikes...and this is a form of self-empowerment! When Doug is able to bring himself into self-awareness, he recognizes how the stress makes him feel. Then he turns his attention to how his body reacts under stress. Then he acknowledges that his stress-response habit is not a "good trait."

Labeling Stress

When you are spiraling into stress, it can be challenging to take a moment to stop and reflect. So, let's try it now, while you're calm. Identify a moment in the past when you were struggling with stress. Do your best to take yourself back to that moment.

Describe the situation.

_____

_____

_____

_____

_____

Describe where in your body you feel the stress.

_____

_____

_____

_____

Describe the feelings rising from this situation.

_____

_____

_____

_____

During times of crisis, you may experience some negative emotions that you're not sure what to do with. You might even hold them in such a negative space that you feel as if you can't even identify what you're feeling.

Check out the box of emotions below. Knowing your emotions is critical to regaining control and a critical step toward self-empowerment. Circle any emotion you might feel when you are in an intensely stressful situation.

BOX OF EMOTIONS

ANGER	ANXIETY	HOPELESSNESS
FRUSTRATION	SADNESS	WITHDRAWAL
IRRITATION	WORRY	NUMBNESS
FEAR	DISGUST	APATHY

We call this a "box of emotions," as you yourself may feel boxed in by uncomfortable feelings that you don't know what the heck to do with. Labeling your emotional distress in a mindful manner will help you push yourself out of that box and put you onto your path of self-empowerment.

De-stress the Mess

Now that you've spent some time labeling your emotions, it's important to know that these negative emotions can sometimes sit within us and be a part of our daily experience. Hey, you're only human, and that's part of the human condition. But instead of fixating on these negative emotions, the following activity can help you replace them with more mindfully positive ways to challenge a stressful crisis and move you into the realm of self-empowerment. Think about this:

What negative emotions did you circle as prominent in the Box of Emotions?

_____

_____

What positive emotions, rather than negative emotions, would you prefer to be feeling?

_____

_____

What can you do to redirect your negative emotions into more mindfully positive emotions?

_____

_____

_____

_____

It's okay if you don't know how to redirect your negative emotions. We have some ideas for you! 😃 The next few times you feel a strong negative emotion, pick a de-stressing activity and do it. Each time try a different one, until you've tried them all.

Place a checkmark next to each activity as you complete it.

DE-STRESSING ACTIVITY	CHECK EACH TIME YOU COMPLETE
Stretch	
Go on a walk	
Look at pictures of friends, family, or pets	
Exercise	
Listen to relatable music	
Cry it out	
Breathe in fresh air	
Watch or listen to comedy	
Connect with nature	
Other:	

Once you're done with a de-stressing activity, write about it.

What stress emotions were you feeling before you began the activity?

_____

_____

_____

What thoughts did you have during the de-stressing activity?

_____

_____

_____

_____

Did your thoughts or emotions change during the activity? If yes, how?

_____

_____

When did you realize your thoughts or emotions had changed?

_____

_____

✳ ✳ ✳ *These de-stressing activities can help you to normalize the sensations of stress. Not only will they make you feel better, they will also help you to mindfully regulate stress emotions when you feel powerless. But if that doesn't work, you can always Breathe It Out!*

Breathe It Out 5-5-5

Now that you've identified your power through mindful activities, it's time to harness it! When you are in control and no longer feeling like you're boxed in with the bad stuff, it's time to let go of the negativity.

Some days, though, it's really hard to just let go of negative emotions. They can sometimes feel as if they're following you around all day. Breathing these ugly emotions out of your body will release the tension and allow more positive emotions to take their place. Do the 5-5-5 Breathing Exercise from earlier in this chapter anytime you want to feel more stable, calm, and in control.

I DESERVE IT

Even on your best days, it's important to stay mindful. One way you can do this is by incorporating gratitude into your daily life.

Gratitude is showing appreciation and thankfulness toward others and toward ourselves with kindness and compassion. We tend to think of gratitude as only thanking others, but it's just as important to thank ourselves for things like our accomplishments, making difficult decisions, and coping with stress.

Let's talk about *self-gratitude*—the state of being thankful to yourself for the amazing person you are. So, when was the last time you treated yourself? Have you recently thanked yourself? Can you even think of the last time you were grateful for who you are?

* HUNTER'S STORY

Hunter comes from a family full of clashing personalities, in which he feels as though he's not seen. He has assigned himself the role of family moderator and attempts to solve the conflicts between his parents and siblings. But he feels like his attempts to mediate make his relationships with his family worse, not better.

6 6 I feel like my parents and siblings are avoiding me even though I'm not even the cause of the situations that stress us all out. I just wanted to help them fix whatever was making them angry. It's so annoying! 7 7

In trying to troubleshoot his family's problems, he has forgotten to make himself a priority. He hasn't practiced self-gratitude for all the work he's done to improve himself and his family life. Yet he has bravely volunteered to lead his family toward resolution. He deserves to acknowledge his courage for stepping up to the challenge.

When living in a household with conflict and tension, it's important to consider a regimen for self-care—your ability to take care of yourself, the best you can, in ways big and small. Practicing gratitude is a self-care strategy that will ease stress and increase calm. For example, acknowledging things such as *I deserve to thank my feet for taking such a challenging hike*, or even, *I am grateful to be able to wake up on time today after having such a stressful day yesterday*.

Self-gratitude can also help you gain a new perspective on self-empowerment and appreciation of life. It's important to give yourself compassion rather than taking yourself for granted, especially when the people around you aren't as supportive as you might want them to be, as with Hunter, who was his own harshest critic.

Practice some journaling about gratitude now. Write down five things that you can thank yourself for.

I am grateful for myself because…

1. _____

2. _____

3. _____

4. _____

5. _____

Think of a time when you helped someone else out:

_____

_____

_____

Now, thank yourself for helping another person out:

_____

_____

Think of a time when you accomplished a difficult task:

_____

_____

_____

Now, thank yourself for your accomplishment!

_____

_____

Aside from being grateful for what you've done, it's okay to treat yourself to something special. It can feel selfish to treat yourself, but self-care is about taking care of your well-being to manage stress, accomplish daily tasks, and do good for others. Each time you add a little bit of sugar to yourself, you're adding gratification to your journey toward empowerment.

Think of something nice (or rewarding or enjoyable) you can do for yourself:

_____

_____

_____

Is there anything stopping you from doing something for yourself?

_____

_____

_____

_____

* * * *Without self-gratitude—the ability to recognize things in yourself and your life that you can be grateful for, and to honor them—you may resent or dislike the person inside your own body. Being mindful of who you are, and the wonderful things you do, will help you to learn about yourself. It will help you stay grounded even when times get hard.*

Pausing to practice gratitude will help you maintain balance between hopelessness and hopefulness. Finding your stability will help you regain control of your emotions during stressful times. Now, give yourself a pat on the back! You made it through another chapter.

CHAPTER 5

EMOTION REGULATION

Emotion regulation is the ability to assert control over your emotions, rethink how situations affect you, and find your balance. When you're able to assert control over your emotions, you will find your own internal power. Rethinking how situations affect you will guide you toward a deeper understanding of situations and yourself. Finally, determining how to balance your emotions will help you to regulate them and manage your incoming stressors with less discomfort. This chapter will guide you through various activities to help you regulate your emotions through:

1. Asserting control over your emotions

2. Rethinking difficult emotions

3. Finding balance

4. Effective expression for a more harmonious emotional state

Sometimes you might experience situations that cause you so much stress, you're not sure how to deal with it. Not knowing how to manage stressful situations can cause you to have a mix of intense emotions that can swallow you up or cause you to shut down. Either would be quite understandable as a coping mechanism, but could it be considered the most effective way of coping? Probably not.... By shutting down or blowing up, you are unable to express yourself properly and may also hurt your relationship with others.

Have you ever had an argument with your friend where you were so angry that you couldn't get the words out to defend yourself? Either there were too many words bouncing around in your head, or no words at all. Maybe you were so engulfed by your feelings or by shouting or acting out that you barely recognized yourself. During stressful moments, it's not uncommon to feel as if you're having an out-of-body experience. This can be considered *emotional detachment*, in which you may have an intense emotional reaction yet don't quite recognize that it came from you in that moment.

We understand that learning how to stay calm and regulate your emotions during these times can be challenging. But the benefits of emotion regulation will help you to express your emotions effectively, which in turn will allow you to interact and communicate with others with less emotional intensity and more calm. ✦ Wouldn't it be nice to have less friction in your relationships? ✦ This is possible with the activities in this chapter.

ASSERTING CONTROL OVER YOUR EMOTIONS

The first step in regulating intense emotions due to stress is to find and label them. This gives you the power to assert your control over all your feelings!

Hide-and-Seek

Remember when you played hide and seek? Sometimes you'd hide under a bush, or behind a tree, or maybe up above, where you couldn't be seen. Our emotions like to hide too. It's time for you to shout at your emotions, "Ready or not, here I come!"

First, write a list of the emotions you know can be problematic for yourself. We've provided some examples:

1. Anger
2. Sadness
3. Fear
4. _____
5. _____

6. _____
7. _____
8. _____
9. _____
10. _____

Next, draw a picture of yourself showing how you feel with one of your problematic emotions (stick figures are okay!).

Or, if you're more comfortable with words, write about how that emotion makes you feel, and why.

_____

_____

_____

_____

_____

To freely express and regulate your emotions, it's important to notice them. Not understanding your current emotional state can bring forth intense distress. Let's read about Luna and how her stressors caused so much family strife that her well-being was significantly compromised.

✳ LUNA'S STORY

Luna was unable to express what was on her mind due to heavy emotions flooding into her thoughts. She was extremely distraught and very fearful of her mom.

> ❝ I was so miserable because my home life was not great. My mom and my aunt were always fighting, and my mom verbally abused me at times. Well, I was so miserable that I began to self-harm. I did get scared my mom would find out because she would kill me if she ever found out. ❞

Luna doesn't feel like she knows how to share her feelings with her mom and instead acts out her emotions by hurting herself.

> ✳ ✳ ✳ *We need to know what emotions are swirling in our minds and bodies before we can manage them. If we keep them hidden in the unknown, we will never learn the purpose of our emotions, and that can cause even more anxiety, or worse—destructive patterns of stress management.*

Emotion-O Volcano

Our difficult emotions can live inside us like lava inside a volcano, lying dormant until an eruption. When our emotions are boiling at the bottom of our volcano, we need to carefully consider how those emotions could erupt and cause havoc.

SMOKE: The volcano has erupted! Smoke fills the sky! When dealing with a troubling situation, the smoke may be clouding your judgment—you feel confused and not sure what you're feeling.

HEAT: The flames are dancing high with intense heat. This is like your initial reaction to a troubling situation. You get HOT!

TOXIC FUMES: The smell is disgusting and you don't want to keep smelling it! Ughhhhh!!! It's all around you, very much like a toxic pattern of strong emotions that may affect you and the people around you. You will want to get away from those emotional fumes; otherwise, you'll pass out!

LAVA: After the eruption of emotion, lava crawls down the mountainside. Your erupted emotions seep into your whole body, and you can feel overwhelmed by the festering feelings.

Now, go back to the list of problematic emotions and your self-portrait. Which one has caused you the most trouble, either with yourself or with others? Which one has caused you to feel out of control?

MY PROBLEMATIC EMOTION IS: _____

Write about your problematic emotion. How has it affected you and the people around you?

_____

_____

_____

_____

_____

_____

_____

You can find a downloadable version of the worksheet for this exercise at http://www.newharbinger.com/51727.

✱ ✱ ✱ *You may have blown your lid during a difficult interaction as a way to cope and defend yourself. However, this is not the healthiest response. Understanding how your emotions work within you is important so you won't think of your eruptions as destruction and loss. If you do, you may miss out on the new layer—the change that comes after.*

RETHINKING DIFFICULT EMOTIONS

Imagine you've just been served your favorite meal. Each food on your plate has its own flavor. The main dish is salty, the peppers are spicy, sauces are tangy, and your dessert is sweet. Similar to the foods we enjoy eating, our emotions also have their own flavors, the purpose they serve. But some of those emotion flavors are just not the right ones for your palate.

Flavors of Emotions

We all experience a range of emotions, and not all emotions feel the same. Just like our favorite foods, some emotions can be salty, while others can be spicy, sweet, or savory. Our emotions have their own flavors, and sometimes some of those flavors are not what our palate is expecting. Surprise! The spicy emotions are the ones you'll need to be aware of, such as frustration, anger, and irritability. So have a glass of milk (emotion regulation tool) on standby in case it gets too spicy for your taste.

Consider a moment when you were the most heated, and circle the emotional spice ratings:

SPICE CHART

ANNOYED	🌶
IRRITATED	🌶🌶
FRUSTRATED	🌶🌶🌶
ANGRY	🌶🌶🌶🌶
BERSERK	🌶🌶🌶🌶🌶

Clearly, when your spice rating is at a three or above, you're in the danger zone of heat! You will need to rethink the circumstances that got you there to lower the heat and de-escalate your emotions. When you are at a higher spice rating, chances are that difficult situations may escalate further.

Let's read how Mila's experiences and emotions are escalating due to family violence.

✳ MILA'S STORY

Mila lives with her parents, aunt, uncle, and cousins. She has difficulty recognizing her spicy emotions because of her overwhelming living situation.

❝ My little cousins don't follow directions. My uncle and aunt don't seem to care. I get angry because, even if they are doing something and I tell my aunt or uncle they don't really seem to care and that frustrates me. ❞

Mila also lived in distress with an older cousin who violently threatened her and her siblings. She even tried to find a solution for her family:

❝ I tried to convince my parents to move, but they don't want to because they say that the house is ours and that they should move, not us. ❞

Just like Mila, you may have experienced a time when you felt frustrated and the situation you were in was unchangeable. Think about those moments and write about three emotions you had felt with high intensity. Complete the sentences below to begin the process of how to rethink difficult situations and emotions:

High-Intensity Emotions

MILA'S EXAMPLE: <u>Frustration</u>

I have felt <u>frustrated</u> when <u>my aunt and uncle ignore dangerous situations with my older cousin</u>. This emotion communicated <u>fear and helplessness</u> to others. The outcome of this was <u>I shouted back to defend myself, but my cousin grew angrier. I felt more frustration and fearful!</u>

EMOTION 1: _____

I have felt _____ when _____.

This emotion communicated _____ to others. The outcome of this

was _____.

EMOTION 2: _____

I have felt _____ when _____.

This emotion communicated _____ to others. The outcome of this

was _____.

EMOTION 3: _____

I have felt _____ when _____.

This emotion communicated _____ to others. The outcome of this

was _____.

When you're unable to regulate your emotions, you can find yourself in the midst of an escalation that may be difficult to resolve. To avoid this from happening, one thing you can do is explore alternative emotional responses. Go back to the spicy emotions you just wrote about and think of some different emotional responses to prevent the negative outcomes you just shared. Rethinking these difficult emotions will help you regulate them. Let's find alternatives in the next activity.

Rewriting High-Intensity Emotions

REWRITING MILA'S EXAMPLE: <u>Frustration</u>

If I changed my emotional response from <u>frustration</u> to <u>calm</u> by <u>asking for support</u>, I would've changed the outcome from <u>being yelled at by my cousin</u> to <u>feeling safer in my own home</u>.

Write about three emotions that have brought you peace and complete the sentences below:

REWRITE OF EMOTION 1: _____

If I changed my emotional response from _____

to _____ by _____,

I would've changed the outcome from _____

to _____.

REWRITE OF EMOTION 2: _____

If I changed my emotional response from _____

to _____ by _____,

I would've changed the outcome from _____

to _____.

REWRITE OF EMOTION 3: _____

If I changed my emotional response from _____

to _____ by _____,

I would've changed the outcome from _____

to _____.

You can find a downloadable version of the worksheet for this exercise at http://www.newharbinger.com/51727.

✱ ✱ ✱ *Notice that peaceful emotions can help you rethink difficult situations with a clearer mind. You won't know how spicy the chili pepper is until you bite into it! Building self-awareness through rethinking your difficult emotional responses will support a calmer mindstate and the ability to stay in control.*

#GOALS

Now that you're building self-awareness and rethinking your responses to your emotions, let's demonstrate that knowledge through creating goals. Why do you need goals? Goals can be motivational tools to help you administer change for a better outcome. However, goals can also get tricky, especially when you're not sure how to start the race or cross the finish line.

✱ BELLA'S STORY

Bella had been bullied both at school by peers and at home by family members.

> ❝ Each day I felt trapped. I felt like a soldier going into battle every morning as I went to school because these girls would make fun of me constantly. I felt really insecure. People would come up to me and ask me why I was so shy and quiet. I am not shy or quiet. I wasn't myself at all in middle school. How would you feel not being yourself for a lot of time? For me it felt like hell. I was in a very bad state of mind. Every single day I went to school, I just wanted to get it over with. I was not living my life as well or as I wanted it to be. ❞

Notice how Bella didn't have any goals for her emotional responses to stressful experiences. Being proactive by creating *emotion goals* keeps you from getting stuck in not knowing how to solve your problems.

In other words, before you get lost in your intense emotions, you'll want to define some goals for managing them.

My Emotion Goals

MY PROBLEMATIC EMOTION IS _____

_____

THIS EMOTION OCCURS _____ TIMES PER WEEK.

MY GOAL IS FOR THIS EMOTION TO OCCUR _____ TIMES PER WEEK.

I AM WILLING TO DO _____

TO REDUCE THE FREQUENCY OF THIS EMOTION.

THE UPSIDE OF ACHIEVING THIS EMOTION GOAL IS _____

_____

I WANT TO BE SUCCESSFUL WITH THIS GOAL BECAUSE _____

_____

_____

_____

ME TREE

It's important to consider who you can turn to in times of emotional distress before you feel out of control or have a stress-related crisis. So let's create your *Me Tree* of life support to identify who you can talk to before you feel so overwhelmed that you lose control of your emotions. Keep in mind that support networks are made up of people who listen to you and provide a space that feels safe to discuss your difficult emotions. Your supporters can offer you opportunities for growth that will help you further develop into the wonderful person you can become. Support networks should allow you to share both your good and bad sides with no judgment or ill intentions.

1. Trace your hand, including your wrist. Make sure to leave your fingertips open so you can draw long branches and leaves.

2. Draw branches extending from your fingertips, leaving room for lots of leaves.

3. Draw large leaves at the end of your branches so that you can write, doodle, or draw inside them.

4. Add soil to the bottom of your tree.

This is what your tree should look like now:

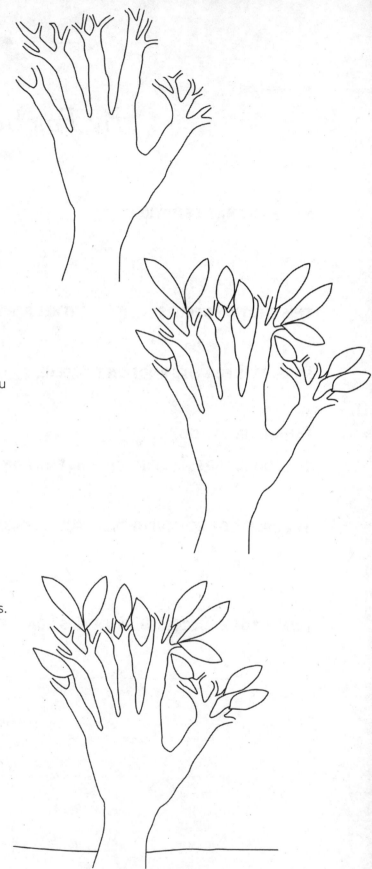

Check out our example drawn by a teen research advisor who works alongside Wilson and Dr. G in their Adolescent Stress and Wellness Research Lab.

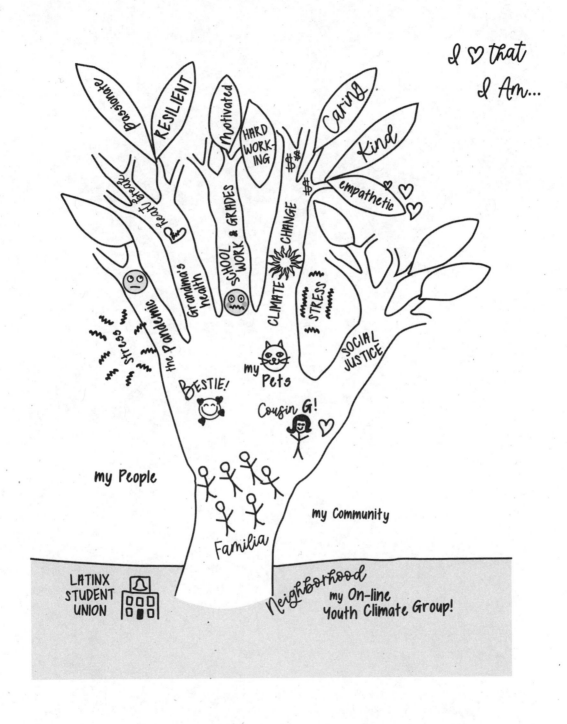

ME TREE

The four sections of your tree—the soil, trunk, branches, and leaves—will all represent support systems you can rely on in time of need. Reflect on your support systems as described below and doodle, draw, or write in each section.

SOIL: "My community supports are..." Consider the larger community settings where you can find support.

TRUNK: "The people who can support me are..." Consider family, friends, mentors, and others, who you feel you can turn to for support.

BRANCHES: "My stressors are..." Reflect on the issues that cause you so much stress that you feel a loss of emotional control. These are the things you will want to share with your support system when in need.

LEAVES: "I love that I am..." Reflect on your strengths that help support you. When you're feeling overwhelmed, tap into your strengths and believe in your own power to find your calm.

Get creative! Add color, fabric, or other decorations to your Me Tree. Once you're done, your tree could look something like this:

You might feel you don't have enough of a support system, but that doesn't mean you're alone. In a world with countless ways to connect to others in person or virtually, there are many different outlets to build a support network around yourself. Notice how our teen research advisor included her online climate concern group.

✱ ✱ ✱ *Art is a form of self-exploration that helps to put you in a zone of calm and ease. Consider this an emotion-soothing activity all its own.*

FINDING BALANCE

We understand that many situations can complicate how you feel. But you want to be careful not to start off with a high intensity of emotion because escalations will only go up from there. So, start by checking in with your emotions, then use strategies from this book to keep you as emotionally balanced as possible. If you enter a stressful situation with a volatile approach, you run the risk of self-sabotaging important relationships and friendships as well as your own well-being.

Red Light! Green Light!

Use our method below (BOP-2-TOP) to help you regain emotional balance when you're feeling as if you're about to burst. A good pause, reflection, and thoughtful response will help you when your emotions are intense and you're afraid you might lose control.

Let's think back to the Emotion-O Volcano activity. You identified your problematic emotions that were broiling inside of you; now utilize those emotions for this next activity.

● **BREATHE** Close your eyes and take a pause in your mind and body. Take a long, deep breath. Breathe in...breathe out. This initiates your RED LIGHT! (STOP!)

Is your breathing quick? Slow? Erratic?

_____

Keep breathing a little deeper and slower. Focusing on your breath will help you to pay attention to something other than the stress situation that is causing your emotions to escalate.

How has regulating your breathing helped you to regain calm and composure?

_____

_____

_____

OPEN YOUR MIND Clear your mind of the thoughts that race after a stressful situation. Identify those negative thoughts.

What thoughts are swirling in your mind?

_____

_____

_____

_____

PAUSE Reflect on yourself for a moment. Take some time to notice what urges you may have and how you're feeling.

What is it that you are reacting to?

_____

_____

_____

_____

What do you instinctively want to do?

_____

_____

_____

_____

● **TIME 2 CHECK IN** You may start to feel overwhelmed by your self-reflection. This is a good time to check in on your breathing. Take in another deep breath and answer:

What differences are you starting to notice in how you feel and respond to the situation?

_____

_____

_____

● **THINK** Consider unhealthy reactions that cause distress and disruptions. Think about the disruptive thoughts you had in the past that caused more distress for you and others.

What destructive thoughts must you let go of?

_____

_____

_____

Which thoughts can serve you?

_____

_____

_____

● **OUTCOME** Take some perspective on what just happened and why you're reacting. It's time to apply a new and different method to resolve a difficult situation. This can be tricky, but you can do it. Move forward and away from the emotional intensity. Yes! You can choose a new outcome: emotion regulation. This is your GREEN LIGHT! (GO!)

What is the bigger picture of what's going on?

_____

_____

_____

Is there another reasonable explanation as to why this situation occurred?

_____

_____

How much will this situation affect you right now? What do you think the outcome will be?

_____

_____

How much will this situation affect you six months from now?

_____

_____

🌑 **PRAISE** Look at you go! You just applied a new strategy to help de-escalate intense emotions. It's important to give yourself praise when setting a new standard for yourself. It was challenging, but you got through it.

The best thing I just did for myself right now is: _____

_____

I am proud of myself because: _____

_____

✱ ✱ ✱ _When you get to this step, be proud about learning how to think differently and do something other than what your emotions want you to do. For the sake of your body and emotional balance, you can choose a new response._

Let's take a look at how Malik's stressors caused emotional escalation when faced with his parents' bickering and his struggles to find balance.

✱ MALIK'S STORY

Malik is a freshman in high school who has been dealing with a lot of family conflict. He wants to resolve his parents' issues since he notices his mental health declining.

> 66 It frustrates me a lot when my dad argues with my mom because I know there is nothing I can do. My mom gets me more stressed because she does not do anything about it and usually shuts me up when I try to talk to her about it. My mom and dad have a complicated relationship. I have talked to my mom about getting a divorce, but my mom is stubborn and won't do it, because she doesn't want the stress. I usually get angry with my mom about her not dealing with her situation and saying it's not my business. The complicated situation makes me depressed to a point where I can't stop thinking about it and just stress about what a bad life I have. 99

Malik was so caught up with his parents' issues that he dismissed taking care of his own mental health. He had invested most of his time in solving his mother's problems, and understandably so! Advocacy for family members is important, yet it can also create an emotional imbalance. Malik could benefit from taking a moment to cool down before jumping straight in to solve a problem.

✱ ✱ ✱ *Emotions are good for us—that's why we have them! However, when in a setting where emotions are heightened, our reactions can keep us from finding balanced solutions to the problem at hand. Breathing through an emotional red light will help you to regain control and regulate your feelings.*

EFFECTIVE EXPRESSION

Rapidly changing intense emotions can damage important relationships with friends and loved ones. We don't want that for you! Especially since we know that volatility can be soothed with good emotion-regulation strategies. You may not believe us yet, but practicing regulation strategies through *effective expression* will help you to better control your various emotional states when interacting with others during intense situations.

✳ ANYA'S STORY

Anya is a sixteen-year-old junior in high school and recently lost her father. Her father had made a strong imprint on her to always be happy. Now with her father's passing, she is unable to find a space to be happy. She is doing her best to cope, but her mixture of emotions is interfering with her ability to stick to just one emotion at a time.

> I have my good days and my bad days. I still cry almost every day due to the fact that I miss him a lot. I try to make him proud, but sometimes it's just so hard and I break down because I still can't believe he is gone. My friends have seen changes in me. I'm not the same girl I used to be before he passed away.

Anya had many difficulties trying to adjust to her father's sudden passing and had battles with her grief process. Eventually, she was able to recognize all the good times that she had with her father. Her fond memories of him were used as a catalyst for becoming a person that her father would have been proud of. It's completely understandable, when we lose a loved one, that we are unable to do things we once did. However, it is also okay to become a new person despite losing not just a loved one but a part of yourself too.

> I've changed a lot for the better, and I've become a lot stronger than I used to be. His death shaped me into a completely different person. I'm more confident, I'm more outgoing, and I'm more carefree. You only get one life, and I intend on living it to the fullest.

After learning about Anya's experience, you have some insight as to what effective expression of emotions should look like, particularly after grief, sadness, and loss. How you need or want to express your emotions is up to you! But it's equally important to recognize your surroundings and how it may affect those around you. This is what helped Anya grow and mature after the loss of her father. In the next activity, you'll try your hand at helping out another teen who's in distress.

Writing a Letter to Another Teen

In this activity, you will become a mini-therapist and talk to a teen through the art of letter writing. After all, the best way to learn about something is by teaching others! Pick a story you just read from either Luna, Mila, Bella, Malik, or Anya that resonated with you. Then write a letter to one of them detailing your own personal experiences.

Dear _____,

I went through a similar situation where I _____

_____. If I were to time travel, I would try to change

_____

_____

Overall, I was able to experience _____

_____

And I am grateful because _____

_____

If I were to give you my best advice, it would be to _____

_____

_____

Here is a motivational quote that I go by: _____

_____

Your Mini-Therapist,

_____

Writing a Letter to Yourself

Now that you have successfully managed to effectively express emotions to others, you might want to consider doing the same for yourself! It is very important to acknowledge the stressors you have experienced and tell yourself that there will be another day to find new solutions.

Take a moment now to write a letter to a past version of yourself. Show yourself some compassion and validate your emotions with this next template.

✱ ✱ ✱ *Take some time to thank yourself for all that you've done. Sometimes it is hard to see the problem when you are stuck within it. When your emotions are heightened, your skills to troubleshoot tend to suffer. You'll notice that effective expression of your emotions is a way to get out of the problem. Like all things in this world, it will pass, and there will be a new day with new solutions.*

Dear _____,

I remember the time when I was _____, and I was _____

_____

Now that I am older, I want to share with you _____

_____

Overall, I was able to experience _____

_____

Looking back, I am grateful because _____

_____

If I were to give you my best advice, it would be to _____

_____

Here is a motivational quote that I currently go by _____

_____

You did what you could, and you will continue to do so.

Yours Truly,

_____

LETTING GO

We know it can be hard to let go of something that you have been holding onto for so long, especially when your accomplishments are geared toward making your family proud. However, it is important to recognize that not everything is worth clinging to, especially if it no longer serves you. When holding onto something that has a drastic impact on your mental health, you may find your emotions feeling all over the place. Consider the effort and emotional impact that go into holding onto negative emotions. Then ask yourself, *Is it worth it? Or should I practice how to release these negative emotions effectively?* Let's look at Akira's stress narrative to build perspective.

✱ AKIRA'S STORY

Akira is an eighth grader and is constantly being criticized by his condescending family members who overlook all of his school accomplishments. He is frustrated that, despite all of his hard work, he is seen as not doing enough by his family's standards. He feels underappreciated and wants to feel acknowledged.

> 66 I'm constantly being reminded to do my work by my mother, and it really puts me in an angry and upset mood. Not being able to show the effort and attempts I make when my final grade comes really hurts because I get upsetting comments from older family members. Even when I tell them that I tried, they often see it as being lazy or not giving a damn. I'm constantly reminded of my shortcomings even though I am improving. 99

It's easy to see how Akira could feel disheartened when his hard work meets nothing but criticism and invalidation, especially when all he wants is family members to display feelings of pride and joy for his accomplishments. However, it would be beneficial for Akira to focus on recognizing his own efforts and looking past the negative chatter from his unsupportive family.

Letting go of something that has irked you can be very difficult. We also know that when someone tells you to "Just let it go already!" it can actually add to your fury. We don't want to tell you that because your stress is valid. But we do want to encourage you to practice letting go of harmful emotions that disrupt your state of well-being. Let's practice letting go through the following visualization:

You're very upset by an ongoing issue at school or home. You're walking through a park but are pretty blind to everything around you, because your emotions are swirling. Suddenly, you notice some younger kids are playing with a ball. You see it heading your way and it rolls in front of your feet. You pick up the ball in your hand.

What negative emotion might the ball represent that you're holding onto?

_____

_____

_____

Your first thought might be to slam the ball down! Or perhaps throw it far away from the kids. But you take this as an opportunity to make a new emotional connection.

What positive emotion would you like the ball to represent?

_____

_____

_____

As you get ready to throw the ball back to the kids, you make eye contact with the kids and acknowledge their happiness in getting the ball back.

What do you feel now just before you release the ball of negative emotions?

_____

_____

_____

You gently toss the ball back to them because they are not the person or situation you are irked at. As you throw the ball back, you let go of the volatility that you have and recognize that you can't control others' emotions in all situations. You can only control your own emotions and release the ones that do not serve you.

How do you feel now that you've let go of that emotion? What emotion would you like to feel instead?

_____

_____

_____

_____

Again, letting go is difficult. But when you hold onto all your negative emotions, it can be harmful to your physical and mental health. It's important to pause and reflect during difficult interactions to reduce any harm they may cause you.

✳ ✳ ✳ Make your well-being your priority and release ugly emotions. Go ahead and throw that ball of negative emotions out the window!

CHAPTER 6

DISTRESS TOLERANCE

Congratulations! You made it to the final DBT technique to reduce stress: *Distress Tolerance*. Distress tolerance skills can be used when you're in crisis mode. Crisis situations are typically short-lived but can feel as if you're experiencing them forever. But before we get into distress tolerance activities, imagine this...

You're participating in a sports activity (or other extracurricular activity). You and your teammates have worked hard to build strategies, develop skills, and form camaraderie. You all have a group goal to achieve success. The anticipated day of the first competition arises. You're ready for the big event! As the event starts, you realize the other team is far better equipped with more advanced skills. All the planning and preparation your team has done tanks, and your team unexpectedly loses. You experience a flurry of emotional reactions: anger, regret, resentment, disappointment, self-doubt, criticism, finger-pointing, and blaming. How do you deal with all these intense and reactive responses to an unchangeable outcome?

Through the activities in this chapter, you'll learn that you can't always change outcomes through problem-solving. But you can develop skills to experience immediate relief, rather than respond with impulsive and intense emotional reactions to high-stress situations that may be out of your control. You will find that these activities will help you get through an unchangeable problem and minimize suffering. Distress tolerance skills you'll work through are:

1. Recognizing Crisis-Based Stressors
2. Applying Coping Strategies
3. Managing Distress
4. Radical Acceptance

When you develop these distress tolerance skills, you will find yourself more confident and resilient to the slew of stressors you might be experiencing.

RECOGNIZING CRISIS-BASED STRESSORS

The surprise of multiple stressors and conflicts all at once can constitute a crisis and can be quite alarming. Think about this: when you're in a competition, your opponent doesn't make it easy for you to win. They will use surprise attacks and perhaps ruthless strategies to trip you up. Unfortunately, people in our lives can sneak up on us in a similar way and cause us undue stress when we least expect it. It can be particularly hard to recognize emotional escalations when dealing with a crisis. Let's read about Amanda, who was experiencing multiple stressors all at once and who lost sight of her escalating emotions.

✳ AMANDA'S STORY

Amanda was wrapping up her junior year in high school. She had been so excited to complete the school year until her life did a 180-degree turn.

> ❝ I had lost my boyfriend and my best friend all in one year. I was really stressed out and I felt very alone most of the time. It seemed as if I didn't have anyone to talk to. I was also receiving rude remarks and comments on the internet and in person from my ex-boyfriend after he cheated on me with one of my close friends. When I lost a few friends to my ex-boyfriend, I started feeling really alone and I befriended anyone who would even breathe in my direction. Shoplifting, ditching with this new group of friends, we did it all. They really helped me forget about my past friendships. It was fun, but my grades started to tank and that came back to bite me. I got kicked out of school, my parents started arguing more, and it just felt chaotic 24-7. ❞

Amanda was confronted with managing multiple stressors at the same time. This made it difficult for her to tolerate the intensity of the stress she was experiencing when she lost important people in her life. She began to engage in risky behaviors with a new, unhealthy friend group. She lost sight of who she was and allowed her escalated emotions to take over her decision-making. Perhaps Amanda could have benefited from the next activity, instead of ruminating on her loss of friends by desperately replacing them with unhealthy people who put her in harm.

Distraction Action

Think back to Amanda's story and her unhealthy ways to distract herself. Not good, right? On the other hand, distracting yourself with healthy tasks can relieve you from having a harder time. You may not be able to solve the problem in the immediate moment, but you can engage in an activity to reduce the emotional intensity of a crisis.

Here are some productive distractions to help redirect negative, intense emotions into more positive ways of coping:

- CREATE AN ART PIECE
- BAKE COOKIES
- TAKE A HIKE
- PICK UP THAT INSTRUMENT YOU'VE BEEN MEANING TO TRY
- JOURNAL ABOUT THINGS YOU'RE GRATEFUL FOR
- PLAYTIME WITH A PET
- DO AN EXTRA ACTIVITY IN THIS WORKBOOK

- DO SOME STRETCHES OR EXERCISE
- INTERACT WITH NATURE—WALK BAREFOOT IN GRASS (WATCH OUT FOR... #2 💩)
- BE CREATIVE! WRITE A SHORT STORY
- DO A PUZZLE
- MAKE ORIGAMI

Let's try one of the Distraction Action activities above: stretches and exercise.

Personally, this is one of our favorite distractions and here's why. When you're holding onto negative emotions, chances are your body is stiff and tense, and you're stuck in a funk. Stretching and exercise can physically distract you and help you let go of those intense, negative emotions caused by uncontrollable outcomes.

The key to achieving a tolerable mindset is through your breathing and focus on each body part. As you explore different stretches, you can find that each body part is yearning for relief from tension.

* First, take a pause and breathe in and out slowly as you move your body into a stretch.

* Hold each stretch for ten breaths, or about one minute. Repeat!

* Each breath is designated to help yourself find your calm and soothe your stress.

Finding your emotional equilibrium through physical activity will help you adjust from an intense state to a more grounded one.

APPLYING COPING STRATEGIES

When we experience negative emotions due to a stressful circumstance, we tend to blame others, the situation, or in some cases, we blame ourselves with self-criticism. In fact, most teens are fairly hard on themselves when they experience a disappointing outcome.

You've probably heard of the saying, "You're only as strong as your weakest link." That's a lot of pressure, isn't it? Yikes! Now, think about that team you're on. Everyone is expected to rise to the challenge in competition and not be "the weakest link," which is a self-destructive mindset. You will lose sight of the progress you've made. In the next section, you'll read about how Doug lost his sense of self due to stress. But with the following activity, he can regain his power once more with effective coping.

✳ DOUG'S STORY

Doug is in his sophomore year of high school and has a hard time fitting in and feels lonely. This void makes him feel empty and causes him to overeat to feel "full." He's not happy that he's gained some weight and has low energy.

❝ My stress eating does not help my confidence when it comes to my body. I always feel the need to "look good" or wear things that others are wearing. That kind of stress has given me low self-esteem and self-confidence. ❞

Doug is trying to find a way to cope with his stress, but the strategy he chose—eating—backfired. The two things that Doug—and anyone dealing with a lot of stress—needs to keep in mind is that 1) there are helpful and unhelpful ways of coping, and 2) no matter how stressful a situation, it will not last forever. Check out this next activity to understand the different ways of coping with a stressor and learn that the challenges will eventually pass.

Building Your Shield

Having awareness of your various coping strategies will help you to adapt to stressful situations. Let's review a few coping strategies and assess which ones you tend to use.

ACTIVE COPING: Strategy used to actively resolve stressors. Taking control and responsibility over how a stressful situation impacts you is important in this strategy.

Example: Breaking up with a romantic partner due to their toxic relationship behavior.

AVOIDANT COPING: Strategy used to passively disregard stressors. Running away from and minimizing issues that are causing stress is a typical response.

Example: Making excuses for someone's behavior that is causing you stress.

Where do you land on the Active-Avoidant Coping Spectrum? Place an X where that is!

ACTIVE ← ——————————————————————→ **AVOIDANT**

EMOTION-FOCUSED COPING: Strategy used to manage negative emotions (anger, worry, etc.) when dealing with a stressor. Often used when dealing with a stressor you cannot control or change.

Example: Breathing deeply to calm your emotions after a stressful situation.

PROBLEM-FOCUSED COPING: Strategy that targets the source of stress and attacks it with resolutions. This technique includes active, individual effort to solve the identified sources of stress.

Example: Discussing with your friend how their teasing is hurtful to you.

Where do you land on the Emotion or Problem-Focused Spectrum? Place an X where that is!

EMOTION-FOCUSED   **PROBLEM-FOCUSED**

PROSOCIAL COPING: Interactive strategy where personal experiences are exchanged with others and solutions found through shared ideas. Can be used with both controllable and uncontrollable life challenges.

Example: Sharing problems with a parent or mentor who then offers potential solutions.

ANTISOCIAL COPING: Strategy where intense emotions are internalized upon the self or externally expressed through destructive actions. This strategy negatively interferes with all parts of your life (friends, family, school, etc.)

Example: Screaming "I hate myself" while kicking a wall.

Where do you land on the Prosocial-Antisocial Coping Spectrum? Place an X where that is!

PROSOCIAL   **ANTISOCIAL**

DIRECT COPING: Strategy that confronts the stressor head-on, exposing the problem and finding direct solutions. This strategy is effective when you have a high degree of control over stressful situations.

Example: Realizing you aren't studying enough for math, you plan new study strategies.

INDIRECT COPING: Approaching the stressor with a passive or even avoidant response to disregard or minimize an issue that is causing stress. This strategy will not change the stressor and can cause more problems.

Example: Getting angry at a sibling when you're really mad at yourself.

Where do you land on the Direct–Indirect Coping Spectrum? Place an X where that is!

←——————————————————————————→

DIRECT   **INDIRECT**

Think about the coping strategies above and answer the following:

Which coping strategy do you typically use?

_____

_____

How has that coping strategy helped you?

_____

_____

_____

_____

_____

How has that coping strategy negatively affected you?

_____

_____

_____

_____

What coping strategy will you try to use next time you experience stress?

_____

_____

You're in the midst of an intense stress experience; what coping strategy or strategies will you apply?

_____

_____

_____

You can find a downloadable version of the worksheet for this exercise at http://www.newharbinger.com/51727.

✱ ✱ ✱ *Life stressors will only escalate if you ignore them or manage them with negative coping styles. In fact, finding and implementing the healthiest coping strategy is one of the best commitments you can make to yourself on your DBT quest.*

Ice Cube Challenge

This is a great activity to do with a friend or family member as you practice your coping skills. Grab someone, if you'd like, and have fun! What you'll need for this activity is an

* Ice cube

* Timer

* Pen or pencil

Collect your supplies before you move on. We'll hold on a moment while you get them...

Okay, ready?! Now that you have your ice cube, you'll be asked to hold onto it for two minutes while using one of the coping strategies below to navigate this stressful experience.

Circle the healthy coping mechanism you will use to help you with the Ice Cube Challenge.

ACTIVE COPING	Taking control of how a stressful situation impacts you. *(Ex. The ice is not making you cold; you are making the ice warm).*
EMOTION-FOCUSED COPING	Managing negative emotions when dealing with a stressor you cannot control or change. *(Ex. Breathing deeply while holding the ice cube).*
PROBLEM-FOCUSED COPING	Identifying the source of stress and attacking it with resolutions. *(Ex. "I know you don't like me Ice, but that doesn't bother me.")*
PROSOCIAL COPING	Personal stress experiences are exchanged with others. *(Ex. "So, how are you dealing with the ice numbing your hand?")*
DIRECT COPING	Confronting the stressor head-on! Exposing the problem and finding immediate solutions. *(Ex. Squeeze the ice hard enough to melt or break it.)*

Ready for your quest challenge? Okay! Set a timer for two minutes and place the ice cube in the palm of your hand. Remember to apply the selected coping skill to shield you from immediate discomfort, and answer these questions while the ice cube is doing its job:

How does the ice cube feel in your hand?

_____

_____

Is it painful?   ☐ Yes   ☐ No

Do you feel any numbness?   ☐ Yes   ☐ No

Are you in any real danger?   ☐ Yes   ☐ No

What do you think will happen to your hand?

_____

_____

How long might it take until your hand feels back to normal again?

_____

_____

Do you think the discomfort will eventually go away?

_____

_____

How could this exercise help you the next time you are experiencing discomfort?

_____

_____

On a scale of 1-10, how effective was your coping strategy? Place an X on the scale:

NOT SHOOK					A LITTLE SHOOK					I'M SHOOKETH
0	1	2	3	4	5	6	7	8	9	10

You can find a downloadable version of the worksheet for this exercise at http://www.newharbinger.com/51727.

If you're scoring five or below, that's okay! This book will help you get there. If you're above a five, you're on the right path for your expedition to well-being. Checking in on your progress is a healthy way to remind yourself that you are improving.

MANAGING DISTRESS

When in the midst of a crisis, your emotional responses serve as a defense mechanism, or reaction, to meet the stressor where it's at. On tough days, it can be difficult to tolerate your distress because it's hard to manage the resulting escalation of emotions. When it's hard to tolerate overwhelming stress after a challenging situation, you can provide support to others, which will, in turn, make you feel better about who you are. Remember, you can't always control the outcome of a crisis situation, but you can apply first aid to stabilize painful emotional responses.

There are some social situations that may be quite difficult for you to manage, such as bullying and relational aggression. *Relational aggression* is when peers intentionally isolate a person from a social group in an effort to damage their friendships. This form of social ostracism is frequently done in a covert manner and is a form of bullying. Teens have told us that much of the relational aggression they experience comes from a "friend" they thought they had a meaningful relationship with. Let's hear about Adina and her difficulties managing problematic friendships.

✱ ADINA'S STORY, PART 1

Adina has just entered her freshman year of high school. She has identified as lesbian but is having trouble with her friends accepting her identity. Adina's friends started making invalidating comments that had Adina doubting herself.

> 66 Some of my straight friends, and a select few of my queer ones, turned against me, saying things like "I can't handle your constant flirting—you're so annoying!" and "You aren't really lesbian, you just want attention." Those accusations, among other ones, really dug into my confidence and self-esteem, and I began to doubt myself and my sexuality again.

Ugh! Not very cool of those "friends." 🏴 The type of relational aggression that Adina experienced caused her to doubt herself and her own identify. When Adina hears her friends explain why she is "annoying" and "attention seeking," she is dealing with hostile gaslighting meant to invalidate and demean how she feels.

Adina's unhealthy coping process was to attack her own identity and compromise her self-confidence! We're sure you agree this is not a very good way to handle *relational gaslighting*—a form of manipulation that causes people to question their own reasoning and experiences.

Of course, we have an activity to help build healthy coping responses to these antagonistic comments.

Feelings Journal

Being the victim of relational aggression can make you feel hurt, ashamed, and embarrassed. Although it's not your fault, it sure can feel like it is. We are here to tell you that being a victim is never your fault. Ever.

We're sorry that you may have been on the receiving end of malicious gossip or aggressive acts. It can feel very difficult to tolerate the level of distress that bullying inflicts.

One way to manage these negative emotions is to write about any acts of aggression you've had to endure. Journal your experiences below.

_____

_____

_____

_____

_____

_____

_____

How did you feel after being bullied?

_____

_____

_____

_____

_____

_____

_____

Nurturing Allyship

Relational aggression can sometimes communicate derogatory and negative attitudes toward a person due to their membership in a marginalized group. These groups include the LGBTQIA+ community, ethnic minorities, and persons with disabilities, to name a few.

Allyship is the willingness to have the courage to speak out against the dominant group and their expectations within their perceived normalcy. Building community with allies, or being an ally, can make it easier to tolerate distress because then you have people who walk alongside you and will speak up about your concerns.

Through working with teens, we have learned that you've most likely witnessed some horrific aggression and bullying. As teenagers once ourselves, we've both witnessed these things too. You might think, *if it's not about me, then why should I care?* Here's why: Think back to Adina's story. Her friends didn't necessarily identify as LGBTQIA+, but Adina did. So what does it mean to be a friend to Adina? We would say treating her with respect—at the bare minimum—and showing support, rather than dismissing her identity.

Being an ally to someone who experiences relational aggression because of their identity can be supportive to both you and the person who needs healthy friendships. Instead of just witnessing a person in crisis, you can help by managing the distress of painful emotions together.

After placing your name in the center rectangle, think about a person you can become an ally to and how you can support them. Fill out the squares in the allyship activity below.

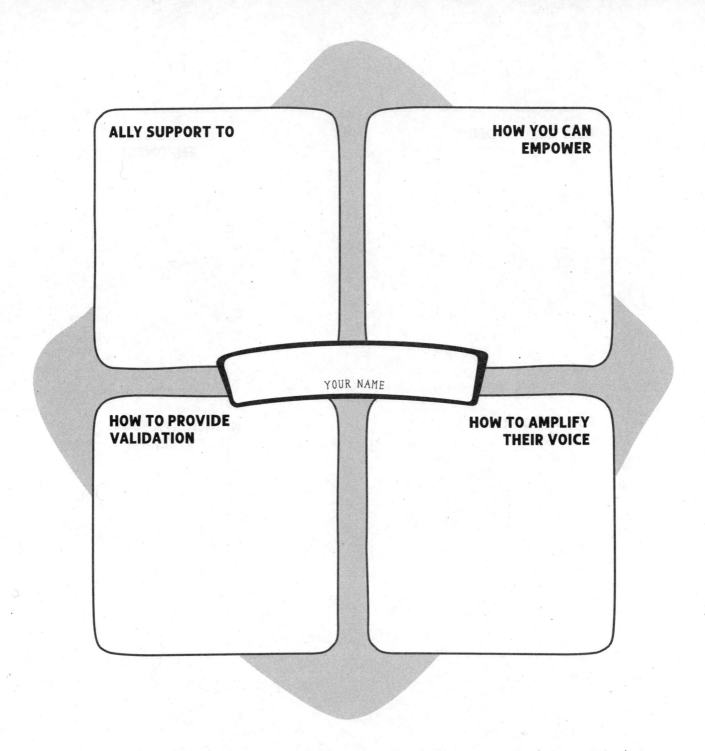

ALLY SUPPORT TO

HOW YOU CAN EMPOWER

YOUR NAME

HOW TO PROVIDE VALIDATION

HOW TO AMPLIFY THEIR VOICE

If you yourself benefit from having an ally, think about who that person is, put their name in the upper-left rectangle, and reflect on how they support you by filling out the squares in the allyship activity on the following page.

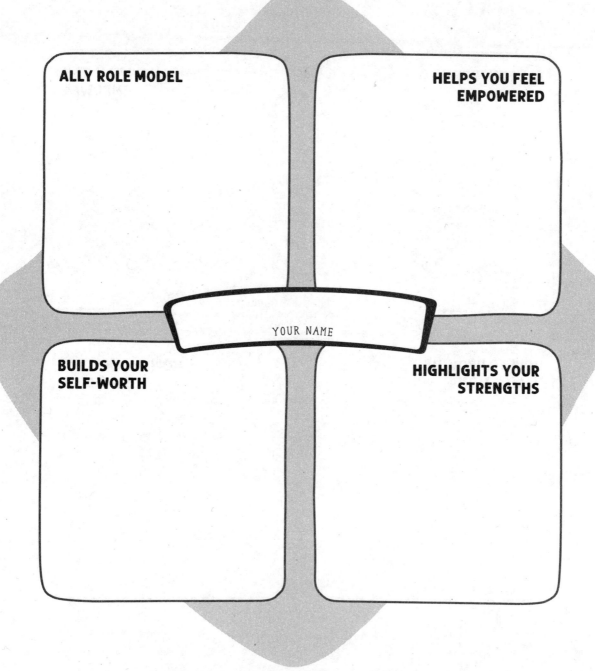

ALLY ROLE MODEL

HELPS YOU FEEL EMPOWERED

YOUR NAME

BUILDS YOUR SELF-WORTH

HIGHLIGHTS YOUR STRENGTHS

✱ ✱ ✱ *Finding strength in being an ally or finding one will help to manage and share the pains that come from bullies and other oppressive groups. Allies and allyship will ease emotional discomfort and pain during crisis situations.*

ACTS OF KINDNESS

Being prosocial by performing acts of kindness for some of your favorite people will not only strengthen those relationships, it will also help you apply immediate relief when you're caught up in a stressful situation. Taking a step back from your own emotional discomfort by supporting someone else will help you build emotional strength.

Read the following story and learn how acts of kindness can lessen your emotional intensity.

✱ TOBY'S STORY

Toby has been feeling lonely after his partner Michael broke up with him. He has been feeling down lately and has been having a hard time connecting with friends. His friend Jim has noticed the sadness that Toby has been feeling and decides to take him out to the mall after school.

If you were Jim...

What would you say to Toby to help him feel better about the breakup?

_____

_____

_____

What compliments would you share with him and what strengths would you highlight?

_____

_____

What would you do to improve Toby's mood?

_____

_____

_____

Now it's your turn! Consider doing an act of kindness to a person in your life.

Here are some ideas:

- Wash dishes for a caregiver
- Help a friend at school with homework
- Take your cat on a walk (yes, cats love going on walks!)

- Pick a flower for a family member
- Hold a door open for a stranger
- Compliment someone's 🔥 outfit
- Share your snack with a friend

Now go out and do that act of kindness!

* * * *Nurturing others and offering prosocial acts of kindness are ways to nurture yourself when you're feeling defeated and having difficulty tolerating distress. It may seem like you're not doing much, but there's magic in the way you choose to show up to support others and yourself.*

Self-Kindness

Now that you've provided an act of kindness to another person, how about doing the same for yourself? When you're in the middle of a crisis, your reactions can be harmful by engaging in impulsive, emotion-based behavior. Instead, we suggest you take a pause and complete the activity below to be kind to yourself and better tolerate that stress.

I like myself because _____

_____

_____

I feel most proud when I _____

_____

_____

Others can rely on me because _____

_____

_____

I choose to help myself because _____

_____

_____

I can be kind to myself by _____

_____

_____

I take care of myself by _____

_____

_____

✱ ✱ ✱ *During a crisis, looking inward at how amazing you are can help you reset your intense emotions. Remember, a crisis situation doesn't always have an immediate solution, so taking the time to provide an act of self-kindness will help improve your thoughts and feelings to handle the situation better.*

Stress Ball

For this next activity, we want you to think of a time when your stress showed up in your body. You physically felt sick. Your palms were getting cold and clammy while goosebumps popped up all over your body. These physical sensations are adrenaline kicking in. Believe it or not, adrenaline is produced because of stress and is released to help you overcome an obstacle. But sometimes, adrenaline can stay for too long in your body, and that can be problematic.

This is an activity you can do with a friend or family member to help everyone relieve some stress and get your adrenaline under control. Grab someone, if you'd like, and get ready for some arts and crafts. What you'll need for this activity:

* Balloon

* Funnel

* Rice, beans, or cornstarch

* Permanent markers or paints

* Whatever stress you have in the moment

Collect your supplies before you move on. We'll hold on a moment while you get them....

Okay, ready?! Now that you have your materials, follow the steps below to help you create your stress ball:

1. Blow up your balloon so that it fits nicely in the palm of your hand. You'll want it to be small and squeezable.

2. Place your funnel in the opening of the balloon, holding tightly to the balloon and funnel.

3. Pour cornstarch, beans, or rice into the funnel. Leave enough room to easily make a knot.

4. Remove the funnel and tie the open end of your balloon in a knot.

5. Decorate it with paint or markers. Your stress ball is ready!

6. Squish and squeeze your stress ball to get that adrenaline rush of stress under control!

You can find a downloadable version of the worksheet for this exercise at http://www.newharbinger.com/51727.

* * * *After using your stress ball, you should notice a release of stress. This is the adrenaline in your body slowly disappearing. Squeezing a stress ball can also help you minimize any painful emotions that might be following you around after a crisis.*

RADICAL ACCEPTANCE

An important feature of distress tolerance in DBT is the notion that we must accept difficult events, circumstances, and even people that we cannot change. *Radical acceptance* is exactly what it sounds like: to wholeheartedly embrace challenging circumstances for what they are. You don't have control over certain situations, so you must radically accept the changes, outcomes, and circumstances that come along with them.

Let's go back to Adina, remember her? She was the one who was slighted by her "friends" because of her LGBTQIA+ identity.

✳ ADINA'S STORY, PART 2

❝ It wasn't until maybe a few months ago that I finally stopped caring about who liked me and who didn't, and began to accept myself for who I am. So now, I'm a senior and just about to graduate, and a lot of the teachers at my school have mentioned to my classmates and I that we should start thinking about our future. I still am not 100% sure as to what I want to do for a career, but I am excited to finish off my high school career with a smile on my face and just enough confidence to get me started at the community college in my town. As much as I had a difficult time learning to accept my sexuality these past three years, I am very thankful for all my experiences, good and bad, that have made me the person I am today. ❞

Adina's story is an example of radical acceptance of self. She recognizes that there is nothing that can be changed in this situation. She is who she is, and she went through what she went through. There is no doubt about that. It took Adina three years to learn how to love and accept herself. That's a valid length of time given the process of accepting things you may not be able to change, particularly when you have the distress of "friends" gaslighting you!

We understand it can feel unbearable to endure and radically accept stressors. So here's your next activity to help you find comfort during crisis situations.

✳ ✳ ✳ *Radical acceptance meditation is an ongoing process and practice. You will need to familiarize yourself with what peace looks like within finding acceptance of the unchangeable. We recommend you practice this activity as part of your daily self-care routine to get closer to internal peace and to better tolerate distress.*

Radical Acceptance Meditation

This exercise will help you to reduce any emotional pain and discomfort you may feel while processing the acceptance of situations you truly have no control over. This guided meditation will help you to learn how to accept difficult situations while easing the discomfort that comes along with having no control over them. It's extremely easy to say, "Just accept it and move on," but that's only half of it. Within finding acceptance, one also needs to find peace with what is being accepted.

Try this out:

1. Find a comfortable place to sit—a place that brings you calm and comfort.

2. Practice 5-5-5 breathing: inhale for 5 seconds, exhale for 5 seconds, and reflect for 5 seconds.

3. During the 5-second reflection, say one of the following mantras to yourself:

    ✱ "I can learn to accept things that I cannot change."

    ✱ "I will be okay with accepting things I cannot change."

    ✱ "I will find comfort with accepting things I cannot change."

    ✱ "It is what is. It is what is. It is what it is."

✱ BIRRIA BOWL

Carlos and George were best friends. They'd done everything together since second grade. George's sister was about to have her fifteenth birthday, her quinceañera! George thought it would be a boring party without Carlos, so of course he was invited.

During dinner, George turned to Carlos and asked him proudly, "So how do you like the food?" Carlos quickly replied, "Well the chicken was good but the birria was dry." George was taken aback. "My mom made the birria!" he exclaimed. George was hurt and angry because Carlos knew that George's mom had cooked all the food for his sister's party. He wanted to hit Carlos but didn't want to make a scene. This wasn't even the first time Carlos had offended his family. Was Carlos jealous? Or was he just a mean guy?

George accepted it was time to change his friendship status with Carlos; making a rude comment about his mom was intolerable for George. They may have been inseparable in the past, but George realized this friendship needed to be over.

Building Your Social Circle

For this activity, consider where people fit in your social circle. Some people will fit into your inner ring, while others, who cause you stress, may need to be relegated to an outer ring. It's also perfectly normal to have peers who move among the different rings, depending on the circumstance.

1. **Inner ring:** List a few people you consider to be closest to you, who you would be willing to share just about anything with.

2. **Middle ring:** List a few people you consider close to you but not secret-sharing close. You wouldn't want them to see your messy side!

3. **Outer ring:** List a few people whom you don't feel as close to. Consider past friends (or family) that need to be blocked so they are not part of your day-to-day life.

Here's an example:

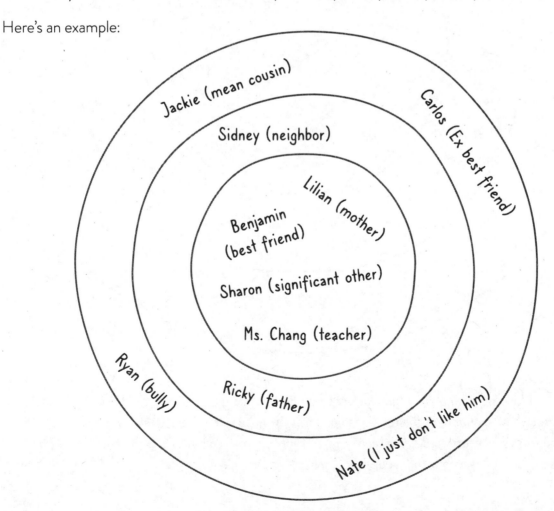

Now that you have a visual sense of how to complete this activity, it's your turn to organize your friendship list...circle...donut—you decide!

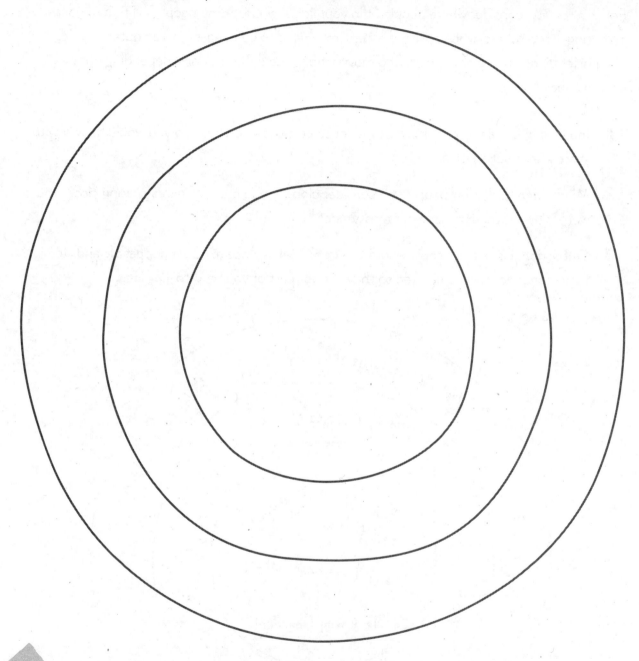

★ ★ ★ *Now that you have a template of who you can accept in your life, make sure you follow through with changing the relationship status of those who create stress and animosity. This can sometimes feel scary to do, but keep in mind that tolerating distress is also about accepting changes in your life—even within your friend group.*

LEARNING–UNLEARNING–RELEARNING

Let's look at these concepts in more detail to better understand this next activity.

LEARNING: To make space for new ideas that enhance your abilities and skill sets.

UNLEARNING: To discard skills or strategies that no longer serve a useful purpose.

RELEARNING: To adapt learned skills into new processes.

Radical acceptance requires you to reflect on learned behaviors and emotions that are part of your existing toolkit. Sometimes, we learn skills that work for us, never having to second-guess them. But when we come across a situation where the skills in our toolkit are no longer helpful, we must relearn our old skills by adapting them to better fit the situation. Yet other times, we may need to unlearn old skills that are unhealthy and discard them completely.

Learning–Unlearning–Relearning is a form of radical acceptance. Let's take a look at Antonio and how his previous experiences no longer fit with a new situation.

✳ ANTONIO'S STORY

66 Growing up, I was never that kid who sat alone or didn't know anyone. My eighth-grade year was pretty great until I had to make a big decision. I had the option of driving twenty minutes from my house to go to my dream high school or to my local high school that was a ten-minute walk from home. I decided to attend the local school I had no real connection to. 99

Antonio radically accepted to attend his local high school. However, it came with internal discomfort and stress.

> 66 Everyone seemed to know one another, they all seemed happy, and everyone was joining clubs left and right. I essentially forgot how to make friends, so I sat alone and didn't talk for at least six months. I did hang out with the popular kids for four months, but I could tell that they pitied me and I hated it. So, I went "lone wolf" and sat alone in the library, which honestly was better than nothing. I was sad all the time and decided to literally give up on everything from sports to academics. I felt like 💩 24-7 and mostly stayed in my room texting friends from the other school. They all seemed happy, and I was mad about that. 99

Antonio got caught in a pattern of unhealthy learned behaviors after a major life shift that caused him to feel defeated and worn down. He became socially withdrawn.

Help Antonio unlearn behaviors to radically accept the changes in his life.

Write a list of skills or beliefs that Antonio should unlearn that do more harm than good. We've done the first one for you:

1. Getting mad at friends when he texts them _____

2. _____

3. _____

Write a list of things that Antonio can do to relearn his old patterns and skills. We've done the first one for you:

1. Check out sports at the new school _____

2. _____

3. _____

Have you ever been faced with a challenging situation that felt like a crisis?

_____

_____

How did you emotionally react to the crisis and what did you do?

_____

_____

_____

_____

What could you unlearn to change your response to a crisis?

_____

_____

_____

_____

What could you relearn to change your response to a crisis?

_____

_____

_____

_____

Learning–Unlearning–Relearning is all about change and radically accepting the new you. You've heard the saying, "If it ain't broke, don't fix it," well, now it's time to fix it with your newfound insight.

Power Up!

During a crisis situation, it may be hard to remember all the new strategies you learned in this chapter. This quick and easy activity can get you through a crisis by applying the skills below.

Remember the words **"POWER UP"** and follow the steps below to tolerate distress.

PAUSE: Pause and reflect on the situation. Recognize that you are, in fact, in the midst of a crisis that is causing you emotional distress.

OBSERVE: Take a look at the situation and decide which coping strategies would be appropriate.

WILLINGNESS: Be willing to accept and acknowledge your limitations in controlling the situation. Radically accept this moment. It is what it is.

EMPOWER: Regain control of emotional pain. Take a breather. You deserve better!

RESET: Negative outcomes of crisis situations are typically short-lived. Repeat the mantra "this too shall pass" at the height of the crisis.

UNLEARN: Ditch problematic responses by re-learning new ones. Ask yourself, *What will I do differently?*

PEACE: Find calm and ease when healthy copy strategies are working for you.

✳ ✳ ✳ *It's common to feel that your suffering will never end during an intensely stressful experience. You might worry that you won't be able to tolerate it. These worries can make the stressor even harder to manage. So, the more you apply POWER UP during difficult times, the more you will be able to manage a crisis or any other difficult situation and handle the emotional discomfort that comes with it.*

CHAPTER 7

INTERPERSONAL AND SOCIAL HEALTH

Your *social health* consists of meaningful relationships with others, good communication skills, a trusted support system, and setting appropriate social boundaries as needed. Good social health plays a direct role in how you feel about yourself, how you respond to life experiences, and your overall mental health. Face it, we humans are social creatures, and we thrive on being in spaces with others. So, for your social health, problematic relationships—those that cause stress when you feel unsupported, demeaned, not listened to, or misunderstood—need to be addressed because they can threaten your well-being.

As social creatures, we also enjoy entertainment either by ourselves or with one another. What better way to support one another than through music? Welcome to DBC, the Dialectical Behavioral Concert (air horns), where all the music is served to your taste and the soundtrack is curated by you! During the concert in this chapter, you will hear a breakdown of the four components of social health:

1. Meaningful Relationships

2. Effective Communication

3. Trusted Support Systems

4. Social Boundaries

Turn up the volume and let's get started.

MEANINGFUL RELATIONSHIPS

Meaningful relationships are ones that foster mutual understanding, respect, trust, genuine interest in who you are, and unconditional positive regard. You should feel valued and loved by the people in your most meaningful relationships. Think about this...you've probably done a little bit of research on the people who create the music you like, and if you haven't, ummm...you're missing out on some juicy facts. Digging into your favorite artists is what creates the connections you have with their music and why you want to listen to them again, and again, and again. You probably thrive on your own meaningful relationships in real life, just like when your favorite song is queued up on your playlist.

Survey Says...

Think about the most valuable people in your life and complete this fun survey about why they are so important to you. This activity will give you a chance to really pay attention to your besties, family members, romantic partners, and peers around you. The more you learn about the important people in your life, the deeper your connections will become and the more willing you will be to solve interpersonal conflict.

Who are some of the most favorite people in your life that you have meaningful relationships with? Jot their names down below:

_____   _____

_____   _____

_____   _____

_____   _____

_____   _____

Now, think of your VIPs and answer the following questions.

* Who makes you laugh so hard, you cry? _____

* Who shares the same interests as you? _____

* Who loves the same kind of food you do? _____

* Who is the coolest person you know? _____

* Who do you look up to? _____

* Who do you want to spend more time with? _____

* Who pushes you to do better? _____

* Who would you want to binge-watch your favorite show with? _____

* Who do you text the most? _____

* Who can you have a burping competition with? _____

* Who's your ride or die? _____

* * * *Did one or two names consistently come up? These individuals are likely the most important in your life. Staying connected to them—and fostering that connection—are important.*

You can find a downloadable version of the worksheet for this exercise at http://www.newharbinger.com/51727.

GIVE AND RECEIVE

Healthy, meaningful relationships typically have a strong give-and-receive system. Think of your favorite duet. Each singer waits for their turn and vibes off their partner's groove. The duet is smooth and the connection of sound is seamless. This is much like the reciprocity you may have in your most meaningful relationships—you complement one another and uplift each other's strengths. There are no back-up vocalists, because you both are the stars of the song and your relationship.

Read the following social story and learn how reciprocity works in relationships.

✳ RUDY AND ROSARIO'S STORY

> Rudy and Rosario have been best friends since seventh grade. When Rosario's grandfather passed away, Rudy was there to comfort her. When she missed school, he picked up her homework assignments and dropped them off at her house. When Rosario returned to school, she ran up to Rudy and gave him a big hug. She gave him a card and his favorite bag of cheese popcorn.

Reciprocity in our best relationships typically happens at the same time. When Rosario was sad, Rudy *gave* her comfort which Rosario *received*. To thank him, she *gave* Rudy his beloved popcorn and he *received* his yummiest snack. Both were involved in de-stressing each other during a difficult time. Reciprocity in friendships helps each person feel a sense of balance and well-being.

One way to maintain your social health with smooth-sounding "duets" between you and another person is to give a daily compliment! There are so many health benefits to giving a simple compliment to people who are meaningful to us. It'll strengthen your bond, improve your self-worth, increase cooperation, and put a smile on both your faces. 😃 Let's practice below!

Give a Compliment

Think of a person you want to give a compliment to, either in person or via text.

Write that person's name here: _____

What compliment will you give them?

How might you feel giving them this compliment?

_____

_____

_____

How might your person feel receiving your compliment?

_____

_____

_____

Okay, great! We challenge you to do this now. We'll be waiting for you right here until you finish. When you are done, just come back to the next activity.

You're back already? That was quick. Awesome. Let's circle the emoji face that represents how giving that compliment made you feel.

How do you think the person you complimented felt? Go ahead and circle what you think they experienced.

Nicely done! See...that wasn't so hard. Compliments can be helpful to uplift your spirits or someone else's. And guess what, it costs absolutely zero dollars to give someone a compliment. They're freeeeeeeee!!!

EFFECTIVE COMMUNICATION

Have you ever wondered why you listen to a certain type of music? Could it be that the beat feels nice? Or is it because the lyrics speak volumes about what you're going through? And have you ever had a song get stuck in your head? *Ugh, that song again?!*

Sometimes our thoughts about difficult and stressful events that happen with our friends or family members can get stuck on repeat in our heads too. This is called *rumination*.

One way to resolve our ruminations about strained relationships is to communicate our thoughts and feelings about the situation. Finding solutions through communication will reconnect you to your most meaningful relationships.

Hear Me Out

We understand it can be difficult to raise certain topics, especially difficult conversations about conflict with the people we love and care for. Practice is key to having a constructive conversation. Let's put this into play so we can turn off that repeat button!

Describe a stressful conflict between you and another person that is important to you:

_____

_____

_____

_____

How did it make you feel to have conflict with that person?

_____

_____

_____

What happened to the relationship?

_____

_____

_____

_____

The next set of prompts will lead you to developing effective communication to resolve conflict with others. Journaling what you'd like to say in advance can be helpful. Here are some tips for what you may want to discuss:

* I was upset because

  _____

  _____

* The reason for this breakdown was because

  _____

  _____

* This situation made me feel

  _____

  _____

* I would like our relationship to

  _____

  _____

Now that you have gathered your thoughts and feelings, let's practice what you just wrote *out loud.* Follow these steps:

1. Find a place to sit comfortably.

2. Select an object, like a stuffed animal, a blanket, or a picture of the person you're in conflict with.

3. Set up that object facing you. This object will serve as a stand-in for the person you're going to have a constructive conversation with!

4. Read what you just wrote out loud to that person. Go ahead, no one's listening. You got this! 😄

That was great practice! Let's read about Alicia and consider how practicing good communication could have helped her in a difficult situation with her significant other.

✳ ALICIA'S STORY

Alicia is learning to navigate her relationship with her significant other. However, in this relationship, both Alicia and her significant other have not been communicating with one another, leading to a disagreement.

> 66 We actually recently got into an argument about me talking to one of my guy friends, and he got mad at me when I brought up him talking to a random girl. He didn't talk to me for a day, which made me stressed because I didn't want this to ruin our relationship. We did eventually get past it, and he did say sorry, but I think that is one of my highest stresses I've had recently. 99

Juicy—we know! When we do not communicate with one another, we can miss out on the messages being shared. With Alicia's relationship, communication was misread and misinterpreted. Let's practice another communication activity that Alicia, and you, might find helpful.

Can I Hear Me Now?

Sometimes when you get ready to have difficult conversations with others, you might prepare yourself by practicing what you want to say—just like in the previous activity. But it's also important to notice your tone. You might think you're approaching the situation calmly, but you may be more emotionally escalated than you think! It's not what we say sometimes, but how we say it.

1. Grab what you just journaled about from the previous exercise (Hear Me Out).

2. Gaze at the stand-in object.

3. Open the voice memo app (a video camera works too) on your phone and hit record.

4. Take a deep breath and share your words!

Once you're done, play it back and listen to yourself. Circle all the words that describe what you sounded like and how you presented yourself.

ANGRY	CALM	ANXIOUS	RELAXED
BRAVE	NUMB	MOTIVATED	DISGUSTED
AFRAID	HAPPY	INSPIRED	FRUSTRATED
EASY	IRRITATED	RELIEVED	SAD

So, how did you come across? Sometimes we don't realize how angry or disappointed we sound. If you circled some words that you're not feeling good about, try 5-5-5 Breathing before having your conversation. Practicing slow breathing for a few minutes can put you in a more calm and grounded state for effective communication.

Alrighty, now that you have identified what you sound like, we have a new activity for you. You've done a great job so far in understanding how you sound *verbally*, but now let's take a closer look at how you might *look* when you are communicating. Remember, communication is the key to conflict resolution!

Can I See Me Now?

Now that you've done another practice sesh on what it might be like to express your thoughts and feelings to another person, it's important to pay attention to your nonverbal communication. Sometimes what we don't say but express through our bodies can be problematic in difficult conversations.

Let's look at how this played out for Jerry and Chuy, who have been friends since middle school. They are in a heated argument; without knowing what their actual words are, see if you can interpret their emotions through their body language.

FACIAL EXPRESSIONS: Jerry and Chuy are in an intense conversation. Jerry's face turns red while his eyes are moving about rapidly.

HEAD MOVEMENT: Chuy notices Jerry's face color intensifying. He cocks his head back, ready to respond, while his neck sways to the left.

HAND SIGNALS: In response to Chuy, Jerry waves his hands aggressively and begins to clap out and shout his responses.

ARM POSITION: Chuy crosses his arms and turns away.

PROXIMITY: Jerry takes large steps closer to Chuy. Chuy can feel Jerry's breath on his face.

What is Jerry saying with his nonverbal communications?

_____

_____

_____

What is Chuy saying with his nonverbal communications?

_____

_____

_____

While we can't know for sure what the conversation was about, their bodies give us clues. It seems as if Chuy became suddenly very embarrassed by something. Jerry appeared to be first in disbelief then angry, and his anger seemed to intensify, while Chuy seemed to want to disappear. Did you have a similar interpretation? Physical expressions can appear different ways to different people, which is another reason that it's so important to pay attention to how you are using your own gestures to communicate.

Communicating effectively before, during, and after a conflict is tough. We get it! Let's read about Dexter and how his communication efforts led to impactful social changes for him.

✳ DEXTER'S STORY

❝ Last year was one of the hardest years of my life. I was bullied by my ex-best friends. One of the guys in my group always seemed to want to compete with me. I was always quiet when he would say messed-up things to me. Until I decided I was done with his bs. I began to stand up for myself and he hated it. He turned all the other guys against me and I was alone. I recognized that these people weren't my friends, and so I left the friend group. ❞

As you can see, Dexter was having a tough go at it with this group of friends. But with enough courage, he finally stood up for himself and left. It can be quite difficult to just up and leave a friend group, but when all they do is give you stress, it may be time to reevaluate your relationship. Here's a little nudge to get you moving in the right direction to communicate your social needs.

Chat Bubbles

Check out these conversation starters. Think about what might work for you when you need to initiate a challenging conversation. It will be a lot easier to express yourself if you can articulate how you want to start the conversation for a resolution.

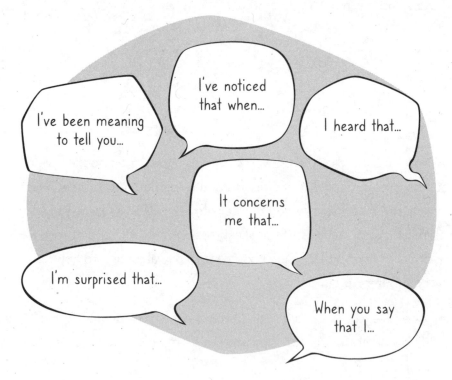

TRUSTED SUPPORT SYSTEMS

Was there ever a time when you listened to a song and just thought, *Oh wow, I think my friend would really like this song too*, so you shared it with them? That coordinated sharing is not unlike the support system you can build with solid friendships and meaningful others.

We understand that your friendships are incredibly important. You may even rely on friends for support more so than family members. A healthy support network of friends, or even a single friend, is important to your well-being. Relying on trusted friends can make a difference in how you feel when you forget to turn in that assignment, get into an argument with a parent, or trip in the hallway in front of the whole class!

So what does a trusted support system look like? Well, good friends should look out for each other and make sure the other is doing the right thing. Friends should include you in activities, treat you with respect, and care about you when times are tough.

DECISIONS...DECISIONS

Choosing healthy friendships for your support system can be a little tricky. It's easy to get involved with those who don't serve you, and sometimes hard to recognize when it's time to get out of the friendship. Let's read about how Ana got caught up in difficult friendships that were definitely not part of her healthy support network.

✱ ANA'S STORY

Ana is a junior in high school who recently suffered a heartbreak. She had isolated herself to spend time with just her significant other during the entirety of their relationship. After the breakup, she realized that she no longer had any trusted friends that she could go to. She decided to go to a party, where she made a few friends.

> 66 At the beginning of this year, I made a promise to go out to parties. I do feel lost because next year will be my last year in high school and I'm afraid my new friends will abandon me. They helped me through some hard times, and I feel as if I have to continue partying with them or else they will not like me. To be honest, I don't want to be out of the loop. I don't want to have them tell me how much fun they had without me. But am I happier than before? Having my friends makes me feel like I'm not so alone, but I still get nervous when they expect me to party with them. 99

At first, Ana was lost, so she clung onto the first people who would spend time with her. In most cases, this would be a good thing, even a great thing! But eventually, Ana started to depend on them for her own happiness, even when they no longer aligned with who she was. Yet, Ana was afraid to venture out to seek new friendships who would better serve her, rather than stay with a group of friends with destructive behaviors.

You might be thinking,, *But Dr. G and Wilson, isn't that a good thing still?! She has friends now!* Valid point, but ask yourself this: Is it worth it to pretend that you fit into a group that would leave you if they found out that your priorities have changed? Just because this support network helped Ana during her time at rock bottom does not mean that this should be the *only* support network that she should have.

Selecting quality friends for your support network requires you to be a good judge of character.

Just when you think you've selected some good friends as part of your social network, like Ana, you might be faced with the realization that a once-healthy friendship has turned into a destructive one without you noticing!

Let's practice what it means to choose healthy friendships to let go of friendships that are destructive. Sometimes, letting go of a friendship can be hard. It's not a one-sided "Should I or shouldn't I?" decision. The deliberation can feel a bit confusing and, well, messy. So of course we have a practice activity for you:

Keep or Leap?

Read the following friendship excerpts and check whether you would *keep* this person as a friend, *distance* yourself from them, or take a *leap* out of their life. But first, let's understand these terms:

* **KEEP:** Someone you want in your life and you'd do just about anything for them.

* **DISTANCE:** A relationship where you need some space and time away to rethink and redefine what it means to you.

* **LEAP:** This relationship is no longer worth keeping; it doesn't serve you anymore, and it's more trouble than it's worth.

Joe didn't study for the math quiz. He asks Davis if he can help him cheat on the test. If you are Davis, do you keep, distance, or leap?

☐ **KEEP**   ☐ **DISTANCE**   ☐ **LEAP**

If you selected **KEEP**, what might you communicate to Joe about the situation?

_____

_____

If you selected **DISTANCE**, what might you communicate to Joe about the situation?

_____

_____

If you selected **LEAP**, what might you communicate to Joe about the situation?

_____

_____

Gretchen asked her friend Regina to create an anonymous post about someone Gretchen doesn't like. If you are Regina, do you keep, distance, or leap?

☐ **KEEP**   ☐ **DISTANCE**   ☐ **LEAP**

If you selected **KEEP**, what might you communicate to Gretchen about the situation?

_____

_____

If you selected **DISTANCE**, what might you communicate to Gretchen about the situation?

_____

_____

If you selected **LEAP**, what might you communicate to Gretchen about the situation?

_____

_____

Ricardo wants to ditch after-school practice, so he asks Gordy to lie to the coach and tell him he's sick. If you are Gordy, do you keep, distance, or leap?

☐ **KEEP**   ☐ **DISTANCE**   ☐ **LEAP**

If you selected **KEEP**, what might you communicate to Ricardo about the situation?

_____

_____

If you selected **DISTANCE**, what might you communicate to Ricardo about the situation?

_____

_____

If you selected **LEAP**, what might you communicate to Ricardo about the situation?

_____

Maria tells Kevin that Mr. Hoffman, Maria's history teacher, told her, "There's no point in enrolling in honors class since you probably won't go to college." If you are Kevin, do you tell Maria to keep, distance, or leap out of Mr. Hoffman's class?

☐ **KEEP**   ☐ **DISTANCE**   ☐ **LEAP**

If you selected **KEEP**, what might you communicate to Maria about the situation?

_____

_____

If you selected **DISTANCE**, what might you communicate to Maria about the situation?

_____

_____

If you selected **LEAP**, what might you communicate to Maria about the situation?

_____

_____

✳ ✳ ✳ _There we go! You're getting the hang of this. Of course, it's much easier said than done, but let's take it one step at a time. Slowly but surely, you are learning how to communicate effectively and be conscientious in who you select for your social support network._

PREJUDICE AND DISCRIMINATION

One of the main characteristics of trusted and supportive friends is that they look out for you when you are faced with challenges. Common challenges for many teenagers are experiences with prejudice, discrimination, and inequality. Many teens have told us how deeply hurtful and disheartening it is to be the recipient of prejudicial attitudes and discriminatory practices. Let's break down the difference between these two terms.

PREJUDICE	Negative attitudes, ideas, and perceptions about another person because of their membership in a particular group. For example, not liking someone because of their skin tone.
DISCRIMINATION	Negative actions toward another person because of their membership in a particular group that keeps them from gaining valuable experiences. For example, not letting someone share a class textbook because of their religious beliefs.

Prejudice and discrimination can be either *overt* or *covert*. Overt prejudice and discrimination is an intentional, transparent attack on marginalized groups such as BIPOC or LGBTQIA+ youth. Covert prejudice and discrimination comes in the form of *microaggressions*—everyday discriminatory actions that are masked with evasive and seemingly unintentional (or intentional) comments.

MICROASSAULT	MICROINSULT	MICROINVALIDATION
AN EXPLICIT BELITTLING REMARK OR ACTION	**RACIAL INSULT**	**DENYING ONE'S EXPERIENCES**
66	66	66
Ewww, your hair! Why isn't it straight?	Your shirt is so ghetto.	Racism doesn't even exist, so what's the problem?
99	99	99

Teens that we work with tell us that when they hear these microaggressions, they feel bad about themselves, not good enough, and less-than. These everyday, backhanded comments over time significantly increase stress, anxiety, and depression.

Let's read about Jordan and his experiences with microaggressions and discrimination.

✱ JORDAN'S STORY

Jordan had been going to a school full of people who didn't look like him. He did not know what was going on and why he was treated differently from other students. It took some time for him to reflect and recognize that he was being mistreated due to his identity.

❝ This teen inequality has been not just centered in one city, state, or nation. I've seen it with my own eyes, through social media, and experienced it myself as well. I remember this one time we had to turn in work from the week before. My friend and I were the only darker-color kids in the class. So we turn it in and get the full credit supposedly like other kids in the class. Report cards came out and we weren't meeting the standards, so we asked "why aren't we passing?" even though we turned everything in and got 100%. Every other kid that was light skinned was passing with an A, even kids that would never be doing any work at all. ❞

The teacher was confused and surprised when Jordan asked about his incorrect grade. The teacher had no awareness that he'd manipulated both Jordan and his friend's grades! Thankfully, Jordan's teacher admitted to his error, but only after it was brought to his attention.

As you can see, adults can certainly inflict prejudicial attitudes and discriminatory actions on teens. So we wonder...have you ever had an experience with an adult who made you feel inferior or less than? We suspect so. It's important to share these transgressions to help you release the hurt and pain that comes along with these experiences. The more you hold onto a secret, the more shame and guilt you'll be burdened with. Time to let it go!

Discrimination Reflection

Share a time when you experienced prejudice, discrimination, or microaggression from an adult. It's common to not want to share painful experiences, especially when you're made to feel inferior. You might be feeling tremendous amounts of shame and embarrassment. But remember, you did nothing wrong! It was the adult who made the hurtful comment or action. Not you!

Thank you for sharing! We know that it's hard to open up, but we promise that it's important to talk about it to validate your experience.

Help yourself understand this experience by answering the following questions:

How did it feel to tell your story?

_____

_____

_____

_____

How did that story shape who you are?

_____

_____

_____

_____

How could your story empower others to advocate for themselves?

_____

_____

_____

_____

Just because they're adults doesn't mean they're right. It's important to find trusted adults with whom you feel safe and supported, and who make you feel better about difficult challenges.

My Inner Circle

Take a look at the relationship quadrant below. Fill in your name in the center and the names of trusted adults in the squares who provide you with support, especially when you most need it!

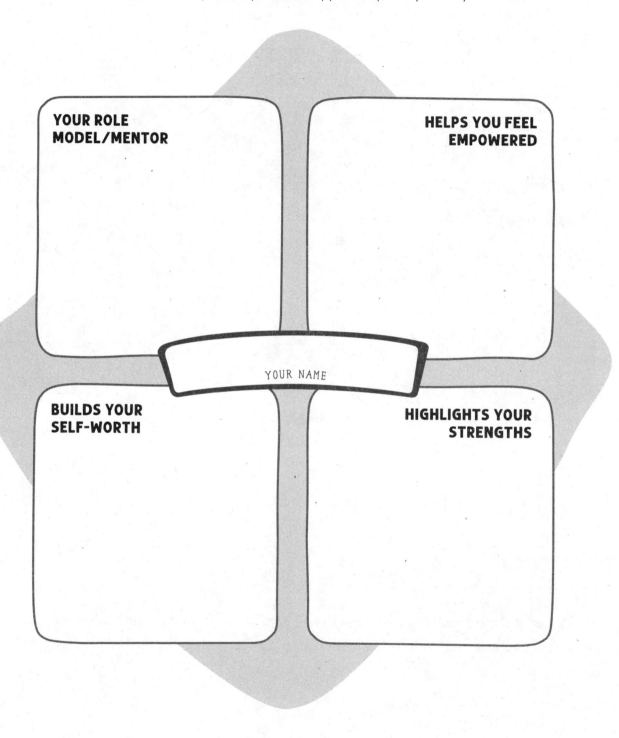

YOUR ROLE MODEL/MENTOR

HELPS YOU FEEL EMPOWERED

YOUR NAME

BUILDS YOUR SELF-WORTH

HIGHLIGHTS YOUR STRENGTHS

Now that you've identified who your trusted adults are, describe why they fit in your inner circle.

Your Role Model or Mentor: _____

How they help you feel empowered: _____

_____

_____

_____

How they help build your self-worth: _____

_____

_____

_____

How they highlight your strengths: _____

_____

_____

_____

* * * *Sometimes, you may not have an actual adult—not yet at least—who fits these criteria. That's okay! Give it time. Relationships with trusted adults can take time to build, and they can change over time just like with people your own age.*

Let's keep at it! Now it's time to add your friends into the mix of supportive and trusted relationships.

Team Me Collage

This next activity is a good reminder of the important people in your life who have helped you build meaningful relationships. We can't survive alone in this world; we need others to get through life! We all have invisible strings that connect us to our friends and family, so let's visually represent those connections.

* Print pictures of good times with friends and/or family members.

* Print out a selfie and put it in the middle of the box below.

* Take all the printed pictures of your loved ones and connect them back to you.

Don't be afraid to get messy with it and grab whatever will help your creative flow! Find your fave pics, yarn, crayons, markers, glitter...fun stuff for your Team Me collage. Grab your supplies and get at it.

MY TEAM ME COLLAGE

★ ★ ★ *We are so proud of you! We know how hard it can be to find good people in your life and maintain those relationships in a healthy manner. When you do, this speaks volumes about you and those who stand with you in your journey toward well-being.*

SOCIAL BOUNDARIES

Although music speaks to us—straight down into our souls—we can't listen to music *all the time*... right?! Sometimes we need to pause a song that we have put on repeat. Otherwise it gets tiring to listen to and the song loses its meaning.

As you've noticed through the exercises in this chapter, you will likely experience conflict with important people in your life. Occasionally, the people in your life may say or do something that makes you feel uncomfortable. Their comment gives you goosebumps... Your intuition is telling you something's not right!

It can be hard to articulate what is okay and not okay for you to receive from others. In fact, it's fairly common for teens to pause and think, *Wait.... What?? Did that just happen? Did I just hear that?* This initial shock can make you respond with laughter, a joke back, brushing it off, or even staying quiet after someone says or does something that feels ewwwwww, ick! 🤢

Solution? Setting *social boundaries*. These are the limits that you set with others to let them know what's okay and what's not. This is an important skill that builds your self-respect and self-worth. *Self-respect* is when you have a sense of pride *in* yourself; you revere yourself with honor and dignity. *Self-worth* is the value you place *on* yourself that tells others how you want to be treated.

Setting healthy social boundaries with others is a form of self-protection that gives space to process the relationship dynamics that are causing social discomfort.

Maze Boundary

Some friendships can be a bit messy with social entanglements. These relationships can get a little frustrating. You may want to yell, "WHY ME?!" And that is totally understandable. The key for this next activity is to remain focused and find your way out of a tangled maze, similar to the way you'll need to attend to your relationships to determine what your social boundaries are.

The maze on the next page represents the dead ends and free flow that can happen in social relationships. Consider a blocked pathway in the maze as a social boundary. Time to focus, rethink your path, turn, and find a new route—similar to managing those tangled relationships. Grab a pencil or pen to get started. It's okay to hit dead ends!

So, how many dead ends did you hit? It's okay to get stuck sometimes. Using strategies to get through this maze, such as using different colors, can help you keep track of your direction. Hmmm, maybe we can utilize that with our life skills too, huh? If only there's something that you could be reading right now that would help you track your life goals. 🤔

TIME-out!

It can be really hard for you to set boundaries with a friend or significant other. No worries! We got you. Follow the steps in **TIME** to set your social boundaries and stay on a path to healthy relationships.

TRUST
Your Instinct

When those hairs on your neck raise after someone says or does something that gives you that feeling of *eww*, pay attention! This is your signal to pause and pay attention to your intuition. You know what you experienced is wrong, so listen to what your gut is telling you.

IDENTIFY
How It Feels

When you are taken aback and have to second-guess whether or not "that just happened," you will want to find the words that best describe how you're feeling. Embarrassed? Surprised? Appalled? Freaked out? Hurt? Identify how the situation made you feel.

MAKE
Boundaries

Setting your boundaries based on how a person made you feel tells the offender what is acceptable and unacceptable for you. Saying, "I was surprised you said that and it made me feel embarrassed" sends a clear message to the offender that what was said or done was not okay.

EXPECT
Respect

Stating your boundaries sets up how you want to be treated. It sets the tone for a positive outcome and personal expectations of healthy relationships.

Let's put **TIME** to the test and practice social boundaries. Turn that music back on and hit play.

TRUST YOUR INSTINCT: Describe a time when your gut instinct made you feel uncomfortable with something someone said or did:

_____

_____

_____

_____

IDENTIFY HOW IT FEELS: How did the situation above make you feel?

_____

_____

_____

_____

MAKE BOUNDARIES: Now that you know how it made you feel, write your boundary statement:

_____

_____

_____

_____

EXPECT RESPECT: What was the benefit of setting your boundary?

_____

_____

_____

_____

Seeing how boundary setting works in a hypothetical situation can help you prepare for a situation IRL. We know you can do it when the time comes!

You can find a downloadable version of this worksheet at http://www.newharbinger.com/51727.

Now that you have another boundary skill in your toolkit, let's take a look at Emilie's story and see how she would have benefited from what you just learned.

✳ EMILIE'S STORY

Emilie was having a tough time with her boyfriend. She was experiencing a lot of stress and heartache in her relationship. She finally communicated her boundaries and how she felt when her boyfriend was not respecting her. It took Emilie a long time to get there, but when she did, she got the outcome she wanted.

> **"** What I have most experienced with such high stress was my relationship. I have been with my boyfriend for six months and I love him a lot, which scares me. We did have a situation where he told me some girl messaged him and he messaged her back. I was mad about it and a little jealous, but he told me and I felt it was fine but just for him to not do that again. I did tell him how I felt about her, because I'm not as close to her as I once was, plus she liked him. **"**

Emilie set her boundary, and her boyfriend understood he needed to honor her wishes. He realized what was important to Emilie once she expressed the appropriate expectations within their relationship. Perhaps Emilie's relationship is destined to end, but until she's ready, setting a boundary to protect her self-worth is important for her well-being.

Reflection on the End of a Relationship

It's important to recognize that fallout may occur in any relationship. You will need to prepare yourself for the other person (friend, significant other, or perhaps an inappropriate adult at school) to cross a boundary you've set or pull back from the relationship out of discomfort.

Let's read about Briana and how the loss of a valuable friendship caused her undue stress and loneliness.

✳ BRIANA'S STORY

> **"** So, I had met a boy and, in a matter of three weeks, I had become so close to him. Before I knew it, I was spending every day with this guy. Long story short, I lost my virginity to him, but he had told me to keep it a secret. A while after IT had happened, I decided to tell my best friend…and she couldn't believe it. A few days after, I received a message from my best friend saying she didn't want to be friends with me anymore since

I had lost my virginity. It completely broke my heart, and I honestly believe losing my best friend to something so unimportant was the most painful thing I've ever experienced. **"**

Briana was surprised by her friend pushing her out of her life. Briana didn't want the relationship to end. She wanted to understand what her friend was feeling, so Briana texted her several times asking if they could meet in person to talk. But after a week of being ghosted, what could Briana do? Sometimes, we need to find gratitude in a relationship ending, especially when the relationship turns antagonistic and awkward.

Journal reasons why you're grateful a relationship is over.

I am grateful _____ is no longer in my life because

_____

_____

Now I feel _____ because I recognized that I need

_____

_____

Preserving my self-respect was worth parting from this relationship because I notice that I

_____

_____

Sometimes we need to let go of difficult relationships that don't serve our social health. We know it can feel bad to let someone go. The truth is, sometimes we need to put ourselves first. If you don't take a shower, the gunk is going to follow you.

**** * *** *Great work setting healthy boundaries and communicating effectively. The more you put the skills in this chapter to use, the more meaningful friendships and relationships you will create. CONGRATULATIONS! You've set the tone for a synchronous rhythm between you and all those in your life.*

IT ONLY GETS BETTER

Congratulations are in order for your well-deserved success. A huge round of applause for getting through the thick of this workbook! If you got to this page, you've likely done a handful (or more!) activities to build new strategies to reduce stress and manage the complex situations you encounter in your daily life. Good for you!

We understand that adolescence can be a difficult journey. We get it! Sometimes you might feel as if you aren't heard or understood. And yet other times you might want some peace and prefer more privacy. Some days you might be in a cheerful mood, while other days you might be feeling blah. Trust us, it will get better and much of the stress and discomfort you feel is likely to be resolved as you continue to develop and learn about yourself.

You've spent a lot of time reflecting on yourself and building new strategies. Now it's time to review. You've learned over one hundred terms, concepts, and strategies in this workbook. So much to remember! Nevertheless, we think you'll benefit from one last activity to improve your quality of life and your most important relationships.

EASE-OUT

Remember when you took the Everyday Adolescent Stress Experiences (EASE) survey way back in chapter 3 and were asked to write down your stress scores in each EASE sub-scale? Time to take it again. Let's see how those stress areas have been alleviated.

It's important that you have completed ten DBT activities before retaking the EASE survey.

EASE – Take Two

Transfer your overall EASE score from chapter 3 in the Take 1 box below:

EASE Take 1:
┌─────────────┐
│   │
│   │
└─────────────┘

Retake the EASE using the QR code below:

Enter your new overall EASE score in the Take 2 box below:

EASE Take 2:
┌─────────────┐
│   │
│   │
└─────────────┘

Progress Check

Reflect on the questions below and journal your thoughts about your overall progress.

My overall stress score has: ☐ Increased   ☐ Decreased

If your EASE stress score decreased, journal your thoughts below:

Why do you think your EASE stress score decreased?

_____

_____

_____

_____

How have improvements in your relationships helped you to decrease your stress?

_____

_____

_____

What DBT activities in this workbook helped you to decrease your stress?

_____

_____

_____

What EASE subscale did you find the most improvement in? Why?

_____

_____

_____

If your EASE stress score increased, journal your response below:

Why do you think your EASE stress score increased?

_____

_____

_____

_____

What stressful situations have you endured that have contributed to this increase?

_____

_____

_____

What EASE subscale(s) do you still have high stress in?

_____

_____

_____

You can find a downloadable version of the worksheet for this exercise at http://www.newharbinger.com/51727.

✷ ✷ ✷ *As humans, we are all works in progress. We have some days and weeks when we are doing alright and everything is falling into place. Other times, not so much. As long as you keep working your strategies to help you reduce your stress, we'd say you're doing great. Progress can feel like baby steps until one day, you look back and realize you've taken a giant leap ahead into your health and wellness. So yes, it only gets better.*

ACKNOWLEDGMENTS

Shout out to Justine Wilm for her dedication to the process of supporting this DBT workbook, from checking grammar, to imparting knowledge of teen well-being, to her passion to help others, and her resolve to see this project through.

Much appreciation is due to the Adolescent Stress and Wellness Research team, who worked tirelessly on numerous research studies to authenticate the voices of teenagers, the foundation of this workbook!

Thanks to all Teen Advisory Research Team members (our beloved EggTARTs) who elevated teen voices that have been silenced for too long.

REFERENCES

American Psychological Association. (2014). *Stress in America: Paying with Our Health*. Stress in America™ Survey. Available at https://www.apa.org/news/press/releases/stress/2014/stress-report.pdf.

American Psychological Association. (2017). *Stress in America: The State of Our Nation*. Stress in America™ Survey. Available at https://www.apa.org/news/press/releases/stress/2017/state-nation.pdf.

Child and Adolescent Health Measurement Initiative. (2017). "A National Agenda to Address Adverse Childhood Experiences." Fact Sheet, October 2017. https://www.cahmi.org/docs/default-source/resources/a-national-agenda-to-address-adverse-childhood-experiences.pdf?sfvrsn=2e830125_0.

Collins, C. C., and L. DeRigne. (2017). "Cultural Models of Popularity, Stress, Social Support, and Violence Among African American US Teens Living in a High-Poverty Community." *Journal of Human Behavior in the Social Environment* 27(3): 215–231.

Dimeff, L., and M. M. Linehan. (2001). "Dialectical Behavior Therapy in a Nutshell." *The California Psychologist* 34: 10-13.

Florêncio, C. B. S., S. S. da Costa Silva, and M. F. H. Ramos. (2017). "Adolescent Perceptions of Stress and Future Expectations." *Paidéia (Ribeirão Preto)* 27(66): 60–68.

Garcia, D. (2013). "Family, Friends, and Neighborhoods: Contextual Risk Factors of School Absenteeism & Psychopathology." (lecture, UCSB/UCLA Speaker Session Series, Santa Barbara, CA, 2013).

Garcia, D., J. Geiger, R. Nguyen, I. Raileneau, and M. Rodriguez. (2018). "Thematic Analysis Approach to Evaluating Adolescent Stress Experiences." Poster presented at the 30th Annual Convention of the Association for Psychological Science, San Francisco, May 24–27, 2018.

Garcia, D., E. Kovalik, B. Cazares, W. Ho, and M. Ta. (2020). "Raising Adolescent Voices: Solving Misperceptions and Miscommunication Between Teens and Adults." Symposium presented at the Annual Meeting of the American Psychological Association, Washington, D.C., August 6–9, 2020.

Linehan, M.M. (1993). *Skills Training Manual for Treating Borderline Personality Disorder*. New York: Guildford Press.

Lynch, T. R., A. L. Chapman, M. Z. Rosenthal, J. R. Kuo, and M. M. Linehan. (2006). "Mechanisms of Change in Dialectical Behavior Therapy: Theoretical and Empirical Observations." *Journal of Clinical Psychology* 62(4): 459-480.

Putnam, R. (2015). *Our Kids: The American Dream in Crisis*. New York: Simon & Schuster.

Did you know there are **free tools** you can download for this book?

Free tools are things like **worksheets**, **guided meditation exercises**, and **more** that will help you get the most out of your book.

You can download free tools for this book—whether you bought or borrowed it, in any format, from any source—from the New Harbinger website. All you need is a NewHarbinger.com account. Just use the URL provided in this book to view the free tools that are available for it. Then, click on the "download" button for the free tool you want, and follow the prompts that appear to log in to your NewHarbinger.com account and download the material.

You can also save the free tools for this book to your **Free Tools Library** so you can access them again anytime, just by logging in to your account! Just look for this button on the book's free tools page.

+ Save this to my free tools library

DEBRA MORENO GARCIA, PHD, is a faculty member in the psychology department at California State University, Los Angeles; and has worked with children, adolescents, and their families for more than twenty-five years in clinical and research settings. Garcia's adolescent stress and wellness research focuses on dimensions of adolescent stress, generational communication patterns, family well-being, and advocacy for healthy school climates. She also conducts psychometric research for the development of new stress measures and assessments authenticated by the voice of teens and college students. Garcia is a community leader, speaker, and advocate for healthy neighborhoods and infrastructure systems for marginalized youth with minority status.

WILSON HO, MFT, is an associate marriage and family therapist working at Para Los Niños, a community mental health organization dedicated to helping marginalized community members navigate through mental health support; and providing therapeutic services to children, families, and adults. Ho and Debra Garcia's research has helped promote advocacy and empowerment in amplifying the voices of teenagers and establishing equality in parent-child relationships. Wilson is also part of the Los Angeles chapter of the California Association of Marriage and Family Therapists mentorship program, to share his experiences and support other marriage and family therapists.

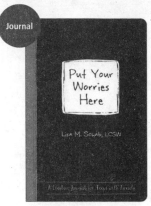